MARKETS IN THE MODERN ECONOMY

MARKETS IN THE MODERN ECONOMY

**An Introduction
to Microeconomics**

Jan S. Hogendorn
COLBY COLLEGE

WINTHROP PUBLISHERS, INC.
Cambridge, Massachusetts

Library of Congress Cataloging in Publication Data

Hogendorn, Jan S.
  Markets in the modern economy.

  1. Microeconomics.   I. Title.
HB171.5.H685   380.1   74–606
ISBN 0–87626–565–4
ISBN 0–87626–564–6 (pbk.)

Copyright © 1974 by Winthrop Publishers, Inc.
    17 Dunster Street, Cambridge, Massachusetts 02138

CONTENTS

PREFACE

The purpose of this book is to explore the logic of the market system as it applies to modern industrial economies. The role of prices and the distribution of income in society are especially relevant in the 1970s, a time when the market economy is undergoing steady erosion as industrial concentration increases and as governments turn more and more to economic controls.

"Microeconomics"—the study of how markets operate—is not a particularly easy subject to learn. Introductory micro texts usually fall into two very different groups. One is the elementary survey of the American economy which stops short at presenting the reader with the theoretical fundamentals of the subject. The other includes the standard college textbooks by Samuelson, Lipsey and Steiner, McConnell, Bach, and others, all very large volumes with a degree of complexity which gives economics its traditional reputation as the toughest social science for a beginner to tackle.

In the winter of 1969 the author had the opportunity to try a different approach. In a series of television lectures given on Maine Educational TV, the attempt was made to present standard theory in a format which was short, light, and readily understandable by the beginner in economics. In the chapters that follow, this aim has been adhered to rigorously. Readability has been emphasized, and theoretical content has been kept at what the author believes is the minimum level consistent with an adequate understanding of the subject.

Readers already familiar with microeconomics will find that this book differs from most other textbooks in three major ways. First, it has been traditional to present the principles of profit maximization via the so-called "marginal approach," involving marginal cost, marginal revenue, average cost, and average revenue. The diagrammatical presentation of these concepts takes up many pages in almost all modern texts. In this book both the average and the marginal principles have been subsumed within diagrams of total cost and total revenue, resulting in significant economies of space and of readers' effort. At an elementary level, nothing significant is lost by this approach, and it becomes possible to come to grips more rapidly with the problems of modern market structures. Readers who continue with economic theory will find it relatively easy to understand the diagrams of average and marginal cost and revenue presented in more advanced texts, having once mastered the principles of profit maximization presented here. Second, this book attempts to show explicitly why competition in markets has proven so attractive to economists for so many years, but that these predicted advantages can be eroded when firms acquire market power, and when social costs and benefits diverge from private costs and benefits. The social cost/benefit problem, as befits its rapidly growing importance in the modern world, receives more attention here than in most texts. Third, the chapter on economic growth in a market economy draws on the experience of Western Europe and Japan more than is customary. There may be much to learn from the experience of others, and that experience should not be neglected.

This book is intended to be a companion volume to the author's *Managing the Modern Economy*, and the two can be used together where coverage of both micro and macro economics is desired. As with its predecessor, several uses are foreseen for it. It can be employed as a textbook in one-semester college and junior college courses when supplemented with outside readings. College students in economics courses using a standard large textbook will find it a convenient vehicle for reviewing the principles involved. Finally, businessmen, public employees, concerned voters, and students of sociology, political science, business, history, or law who need a basic understanding of how the market system works and what its faults are may welcome a reasonably light introduction to the subject.

Thanks are due to Winthrop Publishers for their continued assistance, to Colby College for a grant to cover the costs of preparing the manuscript, to Professor H. A. Gemery of Colby for his helpful criticism, and to my students at Robert College (now Boğazici Üniversitesi), Istanbul, Turkey, who debated many passages of the first draft with skill and perseverance. Any faults remaining are of course the author's.

The greatest thanks must go to my wife, Dianne, who had to put up with weeks of bad temper because three chapters of the manuscript disappeared in transit when the Hogendorns returned to the United States from Turkey. It is said that when the only manuscript copy of Thomas Carlyle's famous *French Revolution* was accidentally burned in 1835, Carlyle used opium and rewrote the book in a few months. In the author's case, the method used was liberal cursing, and it was Mrs. Hogendorn who was almost driven to opium.

To Mom and Dad

MARKETS IN THE MODERN ECONOMY

1.

ECONOMIC SYSTEMS

Markets in the Modern Economy is a study of the economic system in which we live: what it is and how it operates. Although the formal study of economics is relatively new, the existence of economic systems is very old. Even before man came to cultivate land, before he began to dwell in villages and towns, he lived in a recognizable economic framework. The reason why this framework developed so early in man's history, when hunting was the primary form of economic activity, was basically biological in nature.

From prehistory to as far into the future as we can see, humans have had and will have certain minimum needs of an economic nature. These include, in particular, food, clothing, shelter, and heat anywhere outside the tropics. Perhaps less critical, but still economic, are a means of defense against predators (including wild animals, insect plagues, criminals, hostile clans or countries), provision of medical care in time of injury or illness, and education of the young.

The earliest civilizations for which we have written documents (ancient Sumeria, for example) already had a relatively well-developed economic system for supplying these needs. Archaeology instructs us that even during the millennia which preceded mankind's recorded history, these same problems were everywhere the central concern of day-to-day life.

Each ancient society—whether it was strong and rich as Sumeria, Babylon, Assyria, the Egypt of the Pharaohs, or whether it was nothing more ostentatious than a tribe or clan of aborigines around a smoky cave-mouth—faced four critical *economic* questions:

First, *what to produce?* Considering the biological needs described above, and all the less necessary but still desirable goods that could potentially be produced, what selection would in fact be made? What quantity would be decided upon? What kind of strain will this put upon scarce resources? What would not be produced? And most important, for our purposes, what will be the decision-making process?

Second, *by what methods* will a society undertake its production? Even at the primitive cave-mouth, there will be several alternatives available in choosing a technique of production. The skin of the bear can be separated from the flesh by boiling in water, by using the teeth, or by scraping with a stone tool. The most primitive peoples will have made dozens of decisions as to what will be produced. In each case there will ordinarily be a need to decide how to produce it.

Third, every society from remotest antiquity had to cope with the problem of *allocation,* or *distribution*. Among the dozens, thousands, or millions of people who belong to a particular society, what is the mechanism by which output already produced is distributed?

Fourth and last, how are the decisions made that relate to *economic growth*? Will society's level of output rise over time? What will cause this to come about?

These problems have been cast here in the perspective of ancient history. But one of the intriguing facets of modern economics is that these very same problems are exactly the ones that form the central issues of debate anywhere an economic system is examined. The "market system" as found in the US, Great Britain, France, West Germany; the "centrally-planned" Marxist systems of the USSR, the People's Republic of China, Poland, Cuba; the halfway house of extensive planning within a market system as in India, Pakistan, Tanzania—all must decide what to produce, how to produce it, who will receive the output, and how growth is to be achieved.

History has shown that there are basically three different economic systems which have been commonly utilized to answer the basic questions posed above: tradition, direct control by a superior authority, and the profit motive within a market system.

THE TRADITIONAL ECONOMY

The use of tradition to answer economic questions has a very long historical heritage. It is probably fair to say that every society has used this form of decision-making, sometimes for centuries or even for thousands of years. Simplified drastically, we find traditional answers to the four basic questions as follows: society produces what it has produced from time immemorial, with sons following fathers into the same occupation, with the techniques of production unchanged and unchanging (and, incidentally, often surprisingly well-suited to the available resources, due no doubt to a sort of Darwinian selection process). Society's distribution of production is equally tradition-bound according to class and status. Growth is haphazard, dependent largely on population increases.

Traditional economic decision-making survived until quite late even in relatively advanced nations. The guilds of medieval Europe, with membership in many trades and crafts on family lines, the serfdom of the feudal system lasting into the 1860s in Russia, the survival of pre-Roman agricultural techniques all over Europe up to and even into the last century, are all cases in point. Even some family names—Smith, Baker, Fletcher (arrow-maker), Carpenter, Cartwright, Eisenhower (German for iron-worker)—show the impact of tradition on our forefathers when population growth caused them to take surnames as well as given names.

Though tradition as a system of economics is long obsolete, it is certainly still encountered, in underdeveloped societies especially. We shall say no more about it here except to note that, however imperfectly, it did bring many societies through the centuries. But it also stifled initiative, buried talent, kept standards of living stagnant, and resulted in agonizingly slow technical progress and growth.

THE COMMAND ECONOMY

From very early times a second method of answering the four basic questions has had its years of trial. The "command economy" must be as old as the first chieftain newly risen to power who reorders priorities, introduces new techniques, and redistributes income. Strong rulers or a strong nobility acted so often in this way that the command economy in its earlier stages is inextricably mixed with the traditional economy. Following a long line of antecedents, through Pharaonic Egypt and the later Roman Empire to Louis XIV of France, the command economy came to full flower only after the Bolshevik Revolution in 1917.

As the first modern command economy, the USSR will serve as the example for the genre. Here, and to this day in spite of some reforms in the 1960s, the decision as to what goods to produce is taken by those in political authority, in various government ministries which have charge of production, and coordinated by a central planning agency.[1] The techniques of production are likewise dictated by the planning authorities to the factories and farms. Thus a Soviet factory or farm does not decide on its own to mechanize, but will have this decision made for it by the relevant planning organ. The rewards of production are also apportioned by central direction. Wages and salaries, for instance, are established in a "tariff handbook" for all segments of industry and for state farms as well.

In spite of the serious inefficiencies which afflict the modern command economy, and its political difficulties, it is very much a growth-oriented system. Proponents often point to the command economy's record of growth-via-industrialization as its most beneficial facet. Indeed, countries such as the Soviet Union during World War II[2] or East Germany today[3] show that quite spectacular economic growth can be achieved by the command economy.

THE MARKET ECONOMY

Even among ancient societies that were strictly traditional, or even where a single ruler or oligarchy of nobles was operating a command economy, there is evidence that "the market" was beginning to exercise considerable influence in the making of economic decisions. In Europe, it is clear that by the time the Roman Republic left the shadows of legend and entered the era of recorded history (fourth century B.C.), buying and selling in markets, prices, and incomes were already a contributing factor in answering the four basic questions of economic choice.

In Europe there were periods when something of a market system was in the ascendant (Roman Empire in the first and second century A.D.), and other periods when "the market" was relatively unimportant (Dark Ages, say from the years 600 to 1200). But from the late Middle Ages, through the Renaissance

---

[1] Gosplan, so-called, which was set up in the 1920s.

[2] When a whole new industrial base had to be constructed east of Moscow in 1941–42, because the Nazi armies had overrun the major industrial areas in and near the Don Basin.

[3] Where growth rates of 10 percent and more annually have been achieved in recent years.

and into the modern period of European history in the eighteenth century, the market system was coming to dominate. Then, in 1776, the first of the great academic economists, Professor Adam Smith of Glasgow University, introduced to the general public in his famous book *The Wealth of Nations* the idea as to how a market system operates. This is the system under which most of the world lives, and it is the central topic of this book. Incidentally, there are several other names that have been applied to the mechanism which Adam Smith described: "capitalism" and "free enterprise" are two examples. However, the term "capitalism" sometimes carries connotations of unpleasant nineteenth and twentieth century robber barons of industry, while "free enterprise," under more modern conditions, can be a misleading term.

What is "the market system," and how does it answer the four basic questions of economic choice? "The market" refers to the way prices are determined by buyers and sellers coming together in some geographical area.[4] The buyers and sellers will often be dealing in tangible goods (automobiles, agricultural output, ball-point pens, new highways, a new machine for a factory) or intangible services (a bus ride, a shoeshine, a trip to the doctor, an insurance policy). In either case, the goods and services are the output of the production process.

Buyers and sellers may also be dealing in the factors of production used *by* business to produce goods and services. These factors of production are commonly defined as labor, land, capital, and entrepreneurial ability. These terms are not as simple as they seem. Labor can represent more than sheer manpower; skills, education, and natural talent must also be taken into account. Land is more than just acreage; raw materials (natural resources) can also be included in the term. Capital refers to man-made implements which increase *future* output: machines, tools, roads, buildings. Entrepreneurial ability refers to the specialized skills of initiating projects, organizing them, and bearing the risk of their success or failure.

The expenses incurred by businessmen to buy or hire these factors, such as wages and salaries for labor, rent for land, and the expenses for capital and entrepreneurial ability, can be described very simply as businessmen's COSTS of producing

---

[4] *This geographical area can be international, as for oil tankers or passenger aircraft, all the way down to strictly local as with non-transportable haircuts, newspapers which print local news, or highly perishable strawberries or raspberries.*

output. Under the market system of economic organization, any time a businessman produces output he incurs costs for hiring factors of production. Indeed, for any type of output, he should be able to arrive at the *total cost* (TC) of what has been produced. This total cost will be made up of so much labor employed at the wage level then prevailing in the labor market, of land and natural resources at their going price or rental, and of the additional expense for capital and entrepreneurship at their current rate of return. In each of these cases there is a market—for hiring labor, for renting land, and so on.

All these costs have been incurred because the businessman in turn will sell the output he produces on one of the many markets for goods and services. In doing so he will obtain revenue; after discovering the quantity of goods and services and the price at which each was sold, then our businessman will have a figure for his *total revenue* (TR).

A businessman is ordinarily in business neither for exercise nor for philanthropy, but in order to make a living. That is why he will be keenly interested in the *difference* between total revenue and total cost. Subtracting TC from TR will leave a remainder that is the businessman's to keep: his total profit (TPr) before taxes. Thus, TR − TC = TPr, and thus a market for goods and services, together with a market for factors, jointly determine the profit (or net income) of a businessman.

This method for obtaining the businessman's total profit is also useful in determining the amount of income earned by the various factors of production. Notice once again the TC, or total cost, element in the formula. What are costs to the businessman is income to a factor: wages to the working man who has supplied labor, rent to the landlord supplying land, and so on. The people who possess factors of production will thus find that *their* incomes are determined within the same market process just described.

SOME ASSUMPTIONS

At this point, it is necessary to introduce a few assumptions. Assume that in their own self-interest, businessmen, workers, landlords, and so forth, will always prefer to earn higher incomes where possible.[6] Assume further that the prices set in

---

[5] *The assumption may, and in fact does, have weaknesses, discussion of which is delayed until chapter 2.*

the market for goods and services and for factors of production are flexible in a reasonably predictable way. Thus any time consumers as a whole want to buy a greater amount of a particular good we might expect its price to rise, and vice-versa. Similarly, any time businessmen as a group want to hire more labor, or rent more land, we can expect both wages and rents to rise, and again vice-versa. Prices will therefore be related to wants, or to use the term more familiar in economics, to *demand*. This flexibility of prices is also seen in terms of scarcities. If a commodity such as wheat is in especially short supply, there will also be an expectation of rising wheat prices. And if a shortage of labor develops in an area, wages will be expected to rise. In other words, prices also reflect the conditions of *supply* in the market.

With this background, we can briefly examine how the market system answers the four basic economic questions posed earlier in this chapter:

1. What will businessmen produce? Businessmen face an enormous range of goods and services that they could conceivably produce. They will choose those goods on which their net income, or profit, as determined by TR − TC, is highest. Profit is the incentive for production in a market economy. And what goods and services will carry the highest profit? Those which are most in demand by consumers, so that their prices are relatively high in relation to their costs.

2. What production techniques will be utilized? Here too profit is the key. The technique which can produce a certain good of a certain quality and at the same time minimize the total cost element in TR − TC = TPr, will of course tend to maximize the businessman's profit.

3. How will the goods, once produced, be allocated among the members of society? Again by prices in markets, for those individuals who possess scarce factors of production, or factors much in demand by businessmen, or both, will find that their income (wages, rents, etc.) is higher than the incomes of those who command factors in plentiful supply or not much in demand or both. In a market system, those with the higher incomes are able to purchase the greater share of output. Note the incentive involved here, as those earning low incomes follow their self-interest by attempting to shift the factors of production under their command into pursuits where they will earn higher income.

4. How is economic growth promoted? This question is also directly tied up in the market system. The existence of potential long-term profits will be the signal for expanded output, while the prospect of poor profits will contribute to economic stagnation. However, the situation of growth is an involved question nowadays because it is tied in so very closely with government policy decisions. Growth will be considered at length in chapter 15.

THE JOURNEY'S OUTSET

Our task in the remainder of this book is to investigate in detail the market system under which we live. The short analysis of it just conducted was convincing to generations of economists and politicians. But the last 100 years have brought a growing realization that the great advantages which flow from such a market system are tempered by some extremely serious disadvantages.

We shall now begin to examine three related topics in sequence: (1) Why have economists in so many different countries (outside the Marxist orbit) and at such different periods of time believed that the market mechanism holds such extraordinary advantages as an economic system? (2) What are the reasons for thinking that these advantages have been eroded over the years? (3) How can the advantages be preserved?

Questions

1. What are the four basic questions that any economic system must answer?
2. How are these questions answered in the traditional economy? Under the system of direct control?
3. Explain the role of TR − TC = TPr in a market economy.

I.

UTOPIA: ADVANTAGES OF THE MARKET SYSTEM AT ITS BEST

2.

HOW PRICES REFLECT WANTS AND SCARCITIES

The prices of goods and services, and the incomes of the factors of production, are the mechanism through which the market system operates, as we saw in chapter 1. Here we begin to discuss in greater detail how prices reflect the wants and scarcities of society.

Few questions in economics have been debated longer or more bitterly than what it is that determines the price of an object. From the times of the earliest economists, errors of analysis were not only common but particularly long-lasting as well. Adam Smith bears much of the responsibility for some initial complicating mistakes in his discussion of price.[1] He spoke of the value of an object "in use," which he believed could be far different from its value "in exchange," that is to say, its price. How else to explain the very low (zero!) price of air without which we cannot live, or the very high price of, say, a "useless" painting by Rembrandt.

As the years passed, economists of the so-called classical era—David Ricardo, John Stuart Mill, and others—began to refine Smith's theory of price; his theory declared that the price of an object—its value in exchange—reflected the amount of labor that had been expended in the production of the object. This labor theory of value has had an extraordinary life span, primarily because Karl Marx used it in his *Das Kapital*. To this day, Communists still utilize the labor theory of value as a central proposition in Marxian economics.

Always, however, there were the doubters and skeptics. To

---

[1] *This point is very easy to make by the light of 150 years of hindsight, and does not in the least detract from the clarity of Smith's logic, and the immortality of his presentation.*

say that only labor gave value to an item seemed to run counter to everyday experience. What about the natural resources used to make the object, or the machine that did its part in the process? And what about the goods on which much labor has been expended but which very clearly do not result in high prices. The painting or sculpture too avant-garde or too passe, the hand-made coat too long or too short for current tastes, the miniature toothpick scale model of Notre Dame cathedral—all may embody vast amounts of labor to be sure, but there seems to be no necessary tendency for their price to reflect this. The classical economists, and Marx himself, were ingenious in their attempts to explain away these perplexing problems. But their efforts were to no avail except in the Communist world; a famous professor at Cambridge University in England, Alfred Marshall (1842–1924), laid the labor theory to rest in a brilliant career which was at its peak around the turn of this century.

Marshall cut through the cant and the jargon of his predecessors as if wielding the pair of scissors that almost came to be his literary trademark. Like the blades of a pair of scissors, said Marshall, market prices must be explained by *dual* forces at work, not just the isolated explanation, or single scissors blade, of the labor theory.

Demand and supply were the dual forces, with price as the resulting indication of their respective levels. Marshall argued that only when both an object's scarcity (supply) and the intensity of wanting it (demand) are known, will it be possible to understand how its price is determined. In so doing, Marshall helped to unshackle economics from the value in use–value in exchange controversy. For Marshall, there was only one rational way to describe economic value, and that was the price at which an object is bought and sold.

We can now begin to examine the concepts of demand and supply. It would be very difficult to describe scissors to someone who has never seen a pair before, without carefully describing both blades. Similarly, to see how demand and supply interact together, it will be necessary to describe them separately before we see the result when they are put together.

DEMAND

As we have seen, demand is the economist's word that describes the intensity of wanting something. However, demand cannot be divorced from time. It is meaningless, when speaking of the market for cauliflowers, for example, to say that there is a demand for 1,000 cauliflowers; the period of time must be specified, such as 1,000 cauliflowers per week.

Demand can.most conveniently be described as the *quantity of a good or service that people want to buy in a given time period.*

What determines the level of demand? What is at work in the background to influence this level?

The answer to these questions is varied even for any one person, and even more so therefore for society as a whole. But we can safely identify at least five elements which contribute to any particular level of a person's demand for a good or service.

1. Surely, number one in the list must be the buyer's inclination to want an item—his *taste* for it. The greater his liking for cauliflowers, the more he will want to buy. In terms of taste, demand is fairly stable for some items (steaks, shoes) and notoriously unstable for others. For instance, after seeing Yale students tossing Mrs. Frisbee's pie plates in New Haven, Connecticut, an enterprising chap took out a patent for an artificial model in the 1930s. But there was no demand for frisbees until a taste for them developed about 1957.

2. After taste is established, the *price* of the good or service will be an important element. Experience shows what common sense predicts: a rising price for an item will almost always mean a reduction in the quantity a person will demand.[2] Similarly, a falling price will lead to a greater quantity demanded (with some exceptions, such as when no extra pleasure will be obtained from any additional consumption. Example: a 5¢ drop in the price of your daily newspaper when you already get a copy every day).

3. An additional element in establishing the level of a person's demand will be that person's income. The higher a person's income, the higher the quantity purchased of a good or service will be, and vice-versa. This relation is so common that economists use the term "normal good" to describe it. The exception to the rule covers so-called "inferior goods" for which as a person's income rises, the quantity purchased falls. Examples of inferior goods might be horsemeat, firewood

---

[2] *Though in more advanced texts the simplicity disappears in the thickets of indifference curves, substitution and income effects, income and price consumption curves, and other exotica.*

(until the middle class took to burning wood in fancy fireplaces and the energy crisis came along), or those funny 3-wheeled bubble cars which one used to see ten years ago all over Europe but which now are disappearing rapidly as bigger and better cars can be afforded. The epitome of the inferior good is the reclaimed wool, called shoddy, obtained from salvaging old woolen garments. From its use for uniforms by unscrupulous contractors during the Civil War, we now employ the word "shoddy" for any sort of inferior merchandise.

4. Less important on the whole than the determinants discussed above, but still to be considered, are the prices of *other* goods. There are two sorts of relationships in which changes in the prices of other goods may affect the demand for the good we want to discuss: *substitutes* and *complements*. Take butter, as an example of the first relationship. A fall in the price for margarine will almost certainly have some impact (a reduction) on the demand for butter. These two commodities are *substitutes* in an economic sense. There are thousands and thousands of possible substitutes, some very close as with cane sugar and beet sugar, or T-bone steak and sirloin steak, some with a more tenuous link, such as copper and aluminum, or Cadillacs and Chevrolets. But in any case, the substitute relation is demonstrated when a change in the price of one item affects the *demand* for another.

Complements form the second sort of relation. A fall in the price of a good such as stereo tape decks will be expected to lead to an increase in the demand for complementary stereo tapes. Such is the case as well for lamps and light bulbs, electric appliances and electricity. In every case, burgeoning sales of a good caused by lower price will tend to increase demand for a complement.

5. Finally, a person's expectations of the future in terms of what will happen to both the prices he pays, and to his income, will affect his level of demand. If a price rise threatens, he may well join a rush to buy now rather than later after the hikes have taken place. Conversely, he may reduce his purchases today, saving money that can be spent when prices rise. More rarely, if price declines are in prospect, perhaps because of an economic slump, he may postpone his purchase until the fall in price has actually taken place.

Expectations of higher future *income* may have less predictable effects. One person might say to himself, I can spend more now because my income will be higher soon. Another might say, with my income temporarily low I will be best served by postponing purchases until the cash is actually in hand. But in either case, it can at least be said that expectations will alter the level of demand.

The Demand Curve

When examining the manner in which the market mechanism works, the economist often finds it very useful to draw diagrams which illustrate demand. It would be nice if we could construct a diagram displaying the effect on a person's demand of changing any single one of the five determinants—taste, price, income, prices of other goods, and expectations for the future—discussed above. Unfortunately, being limited to two dimensions (or at most to three if we are willing to suffer through the puzzles of solid geometry), we cannot include all five determinants in one diagram.[3] However, this is not overly upsetting, because it will shortly be clear that chief interest centers in just one of the determinants, namely price. In fact, for analyzing the market mechanism, our particular attention will be focused on the relation between the price of a good and the resulting quantity demanded.

In setting out to diagram this relation, we might assume for the moment that *temporarily* no changes at all will occur in any of the other four determinants of demand. That is to say, assume a person has unchanged tastes, a fixed level of income, an unchanged view of the future, and that the prices of the substitute and complementary goods he might buy are fixed also.[4] Thus, in one diagram we can concentrate on just the relation between demand and price.

It was pointed out earlier that the quantity demanded of an object is likely to be higher as its price falls, and lower as its price rises. This can be shown for one person, and one product (cauliflowers) as in Table 2–1.[5]

---

[3] *Advanced textbooks show how this can be done with the use of various mathematical techniques.*

[4] *Economists name this sort of assumption* ceteris paribus, *Latin for all other things being equal.*

[5] *Thanks are in order for Mrs. D. Hogendorn, who kindly took 30 seconds out of a busy day to tell the author how much cauliflower she would want to buy at the different prices shown. The very high quantity at a zero price would be inflated by using it for relish, to feed the dog, to be put out for the birds, etc.*

TABLE 2–1

If the Price per unit (lb.) is		Then the Quantity of cauliflowers demanded by a person in some time period (one month) will be	
Very high	$2.00	Zero	0
High	1.00	Low	1
Medium	.60	Medium	4
Low	.25	High	6
Zero	0	Very high	12
		(but not infinite)*	

* To persuade people to take more than what they would voluntarily choose at zero price, it would be necessary to pay them something. The price would thus be shown as negative.

This relationship is shown geometrically in Figure 2–1, where the vertical axis shows price, running from zero at the origin upward to some very high level. Meanwhile, the horizontal axis depicts the quantity demanded, running from zero rightward to a very high level. Notice that the points 1, 2, 3, 4, and 5, in the diagram correspond to the data given in Table 2–1. For example, point 1 shows that an exceedingly high price has resulted in no demand at all (quantity demanded = zero) for the good shown. Or, at point 4, a low price has led to a high quantity demanded. Points 2 and 3 obey the same logic, as would any other combination of price and quantity between 1, 2, 3, and 4. If data were available for all possible prices, we

FIGURE 2–1

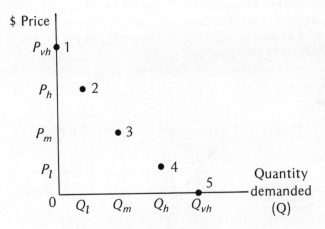

FIGURE 2–2

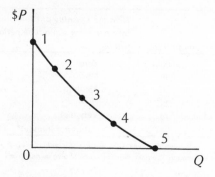

would get so many points that they would appear to be a curve, as shown in Figure 2–2. This is called a demand curve, henceforth labelled D.

One further point. Up to now our discussion has been concerned with the demand of only one individual. Often it is more important to know the level of demand in a whole market, for all the individuals who are potential buyers. Fortunately it is very easy to add together the demand curves of individuals to obtain the total, or market, demand. If two people, A and B, have demand curves for any object as shown in Figure 2–3, then the total demand of A and B together can be found by taking one price and adding their respective demands horizontally. As neither A nor B have any demand at a price of $6, it follows that A and B together show a zero quantity demanded at a price of $6. At a $3 price level, A wants 20, B wants 10, so market demand at $3 is found by adding 20 + 10 = 30, and so on. Finding the demand in any market thus becomes an exercise in adding together, horizontally, all the curves for the individuals in that market.

FIGURE 2–3

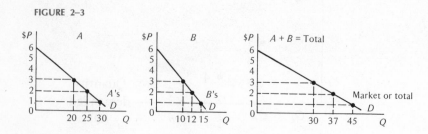

When discussing *total* demand, it should be noted that in addition to the five determinants of demand previously discussed, one other becomes obvious. Total demand depends as well on the number of potential buyers—that is, the size of the population.

Do Demand Curves Always Slope Downward?

The blanket statement at the beginning of the chapter that people desire less of a good as its price rises and vice-versa (that is, that demand curves slope downward from upper left to lower right) has been the subject of much discussion in economics. This has basically revolved about the search for exceptions to the general rule. It seems clear that some people, for a very few goods, have demand curves that slope upward, as in Figure 2–4, so that a higher price leads to a greater desire to buy.

FIGURE 2–4

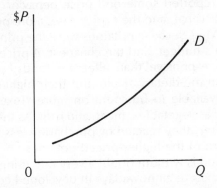

The familiar example is the prestige good, which gives pleasure in part because of its high price. Thorstein Veblen of the University of Chicago first described this idea early in the century. He called it "conspicuous consumption" in his famous book, *The Theory of the Leisure Class* (1899).[6] Veblen first ad-

---

[6] See Heilbroner, *The Worldly Philosophers*. *Veblen was a terribly unorthodox character for his time, alienated, sloppily dressed, a sadistic practical joker, who automatically gave all students good and bad a C, and who lost more than one job for "dating" the coeds. One is tempted to remark that he would have been a big hit at college in the 1970s.*

vanced the idea that high-class merchandise which is not in demand at a low price may become the rage at a high price. Fashions and cosmetics seem to be excellent examples. A recent article in a newsmagazine discussed the race to become the highest priced beauty cream in order to appeal to this type of consumer. The cream named Re-Nutriv, selling for $115 in the one-pound economy size, found itself overtaken by Novessence, whose 11½ oz. jar went for $150.[7]

However, though demand curves do no doubt slope upward for prestige goods for a large number of individuals, a far greater number of consumers would look at the situation in more sensible terms. Thus for the beauty cream market as a whole the curve would still slope downward.

The only market-wide "upward-slope" exception must thus be looked for in an entirely different area, the so-called "Giffen good." Sir Francis Giffen, a 19th century British economist, found an unusual economic effect during the great Irish potato famine of 1845–49. During this abysmal period, when air-borne spores turned potatoes overnight into a black and rotting mass in a country that was overwhelmingly dependent on them for food, Giffen reported some odd price behavior. As potatoes became more scarce, and their price rose, *more* potatoes were demanded! Why? Because potatoes were the principal item in the consumer's budget, and the cheapest. A price rise still left potatoes less expensive than alternate foods, so they continued to form the dietary staple. But their higher cost meant less money available to be spent on more "luxurious" commodities such as vegetables, meat, and fruit. As this left people relatively poorer, they reacted by purchasing less of these luxuries and more of the higher-priced potatoes.

A Giffen good is without doubt a very rare thing, and probably does not exist at all nowadays in developed countries. But in the world's less-developed countries where one cheap foodstuff forms the central part of the diet for the majority of the population (for instance, rice in Asia, cassava or yams in Africa) Giffen goods may yet exist.

One other special case exists where a demand curve will not slope downward in the regular way. As this case is of some importance later in the book, it needs to be emphasized here. Imagine the situation of a man producing something to sell,

---

[7] Newsweek, *June 3, 1968.*

and yet whose total output is only the tiniest fraction of all the output flowing to the market. A good example might be Farmer Robinson's corn from his farm in Iowa. His corn crop is only a small amount of the total corn produced annually in the US. What if someone asked him to describe the demand for his corn? He would reply, well, mine is a good well-tended hybrid, but in all honesty you can't tell it apart from any other farmer's corn when it gets put in the bins at Des Moines. It seems to me that a buyer's demand for *my* corn is a bit peculiar. Any day of the week there's a market price for this crop. I can sell all I want to sell at that market price, and even if my farm were 50 times bigger than it is and I were swimming in corn, I could take it all to market and still sell it at the price the market is offering. Yet if I were to raise my asking price above the market rate, even by just a cent or two, I couldn't sell a bushel. Nobody would want any, because they would get any quantity they wanted from the hundreds of thousands of other farmers who grow corn just like mine.

Farmer Robinson is correct. That is what the demand for his small share of corn output is like. Diagrammatically this is shown in Figure 2–5, where any slight rise in price above the level OP will mean a zero quantity demanded, but nevertheless at the price OP any quantity Robinson has to sell can be successfully marketed. Note, however, that the overall demand for corn as a whole is not going to be this way. For the entire market a falling price for corn will surely lead to a greater

FIGURE 2–5

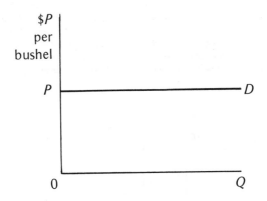

quantity being demanded, while a rising price will have the reverse result.[8]

We have seen that a demand curve shows the relationship between price and the quantity which will be demanded. In the background all the other determinants of demand have been held unchanged—unaltered tastes, fixed income, unchanged prices of other goods, constant expectations of the future, and a constant population. The demand curve for almost everything marketed will slope downward. The exceptions are, first, the horizontal demand curve for output turned out by one among many producers; second, the occasional example of an upward-sloping curve where a prestige good is concerned; and third, the very rare case of Giffen good, also with an upward-sloping curve.

What Information Does a Demand Curve Give?

A demand curve can be used to illustrate many different occurrences. Most plainly, it shows at a glance what happens when, at any time, price changes.

In Figure 2–7, we see that a fall in price (with no change in any of the other determinants of demand) from OP_h to OP_m, leads to an increase in the quantity demanded from OQ_m to OQ_h. Such a movement is always labelled a *change in the quantity demanded*.

The demand curve can show something equally important, however. What if we cancel our previous assumption that

---

[8] *Economists call the horizontal demand curve just described "perfectly elastic." Very rarely a vertical curve might be encountered, as in Figure 2–6. This would show a situation where no matter what the price, the same quantity would be demanded. Physiological necessities are sometimes quoted as fitting this description, salt and insulin being the two favored examples. But the author uses salt on his driveway in winter (or did until ecology scares worried him), and he would have used MORE at a low price.*

FIGURE 2–6

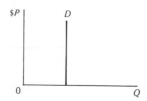

FIGURE 2–7

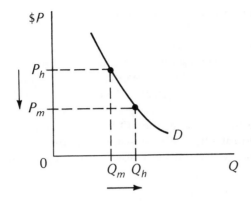

tastes, incomes, etc. will remain constant? Under these new conditions the demand curve itself will be free to move. Suppose Figure 2–8 shows the demand curve for cauliflower, with all other determinants held constant. Here some high price OP_h results in a low quantity OQ_l while some low price OP_l would result in a high quantity demanded OQ_h. But what if one of the following changes should occur:

1. A greater liking for cauliflower (change in tastes).
2. An increase in the income of the consumer.
3. A sharp rise in the price of one or more vegetables which are good substitutes for cauliflower.

FIGURE 2–8

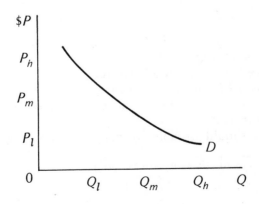

4. An expectation that cauliflower prices will rise dramatically next week.

5. A steady growth in population.

In every case, the result will be to raise the demand for cauliflower.[9] On a diagram (see Figure 2–9), this will mean shifting the whole demand curve over to the right. At any high price OP_h, larger incomes, a greater desire to buy, and so on, will result in greater demand. Where formerly consumers wanted only a quantity OQ_l at a price OP_h, now they want to buy the greater amount OQ_m. Or, at some low price OP_l consumers who previously wanted OQ_h now are willing to purchase the larger amount OQ_{vh}.

FIGURE 2–9

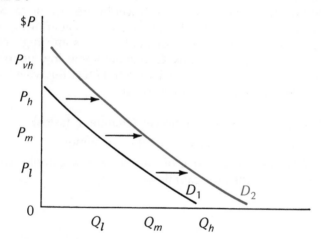

This outward (rightward) shift in the demand curve itself has been caused by some underlying change in one or more of the determinants of demand which we had formerly been holding constant. Henceforth, such a change will always be labelled a *change in demand*.

Readers should be able to imagine the occurrences that

---

[9] *Assuming of course that cauliflower is a normal good.*

FIGURE 2–10

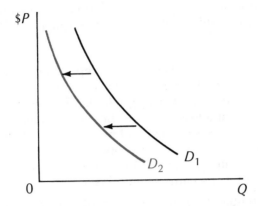

would cause a decrease in demand.[10] They should see that this would result in an upward (leftward) movement of the demand curve itself (See Figure 2–10).

This completes our analysis of demand in the market system. The next step is to examine the essentials of supply, after which it will be possible to juxtapose both of them to find how prices are determined in the first place.

SUPPLY

The concept of supply, the other "blade of the scissors" that determines price, is in many ways analagous to demand. As we did previously with the demand concept, we can define supply in a sentence, note its relation to a time period, discover the several elements which determine whether it is large or small, show it diagrammatically, and finally, distinguish between changes along a supply curve and changes in the position of the curve itself.

Supply can be defined as the quantity of a good or service that a seller wishes to sell on the market. As with demand, supply must be associated with some time period—so much per hour, or per year.

What does the level of supply depend upon? Let us select one company—for example, the Welkin Ring Company—

---

[10] *Simply reverse the examples 1–5 just described.*

which is said to be a maker of college class rings and wedding bands, and located in Welkin, California.[11] Several determinants are present which will influence the company's decision as to what quantity of rings it will produce.

1.   Before anything else, this will depend on the *objectives* of the firm. Is old Mr. Welkin a philanthropist who would like to see every young man wearing a Welkin Ring even though his company runs at a loss? Or does he merely want a quiet life, earning just enough for him and his family to live on? Or, as usually assumed in first-year economics and no doubt very close to the truth for most sellers, does Welkin want to maximize the profits he earns selling rings?[12]

2.   In number 1 above, let us adopt the usual assumption that firms are in business to make the greatest profit that they can. It will therefore be of intense interest for them to know what the *price* of the product they are selling is. All other things being equal, a higher price will allow Welkin to earn a higher profit on each ring sold. The company can take full advantage of this only by increasing its output.

3.   Supply will also be dependent on the prices of the factors of production used by the firm; that is, the *costs of production* incurred when labor, land, capital, and entrepreneurial ability are acquired. Look at it this way: if the skilled labor needed to engrave the student's ring goes up in price, with nothing else changed, then this will cut into Welkin's profits on college rings. However, the skilled engraver is not needed for the firm's golden wedding bands. So a switch in output occurs, and a rise in factor cost has led to a decline in the quantity of college rings supplied.

4.   Closely allied to this, the supply of a good will be affected by any *change in the price of goods which can be substituted in production*. The supply of college rings will be affected by a fall or rise in the price of the firm's wedding bands. A fall will lead to more college rings being produced; a rise to more wedding bands. Many areas of production will have substitutes to consider: for the farmer, corn or soybeans; for the rancher, cattle or sheep (or within these categories, milk or beef, wool or

---

[11] *However, the author will not vouch for this.*

[12] *This assumption is considered in more detail in chapter 4.*

lamb); for the shipbuilder, container ships or tankers; for Detroit, Lincolns or Pintos.[13]

5. Also tied to this, *expectations concerning the future price* not only of the product considered, but also of its substitutes, will influence present supply.

6. Finally, the current state of technology—the *techniques of production*—will affect the level of supply. Inventions (the discovery of a new method of doing something) and innovations (the adopting of inventions so that they are useful in the production process) will certainly have their effect on supply. In Welkin's case, a newly developed stamping machine for rings may make sweeping changes in supply conditions.

The Supply Curve

Just as with demand, it is useful to construct a diagram that shows what occurs when any of these determinants undergoes a change. As before, our study of the market mechanism leads us to a special interest in one of these, namely, the relation between price and the quantity supplied. Thus, with the other five elements kept constant for the time being, we can ask what quantity of a good will be supplied to the market by a seller during a time period, at various different prices.

It has already been mentioned that the Welkin Ring Company will want to increase the quantity of college rings it supplies to the market *if* the prices of these rings rise and:

1. The firm wants to maximize its profits.
2. Its costs are unchanged.
3. The prices of its other rings stay the same.
4. Its expectations of the future are unaltered.
5. Its technology remains constant.

(Or, to use the more convenient shorthand phrase, "All other things being equal.")

---

[13] *For a most remarkable example of substitutability see Chapter 19 of Charles Dickens' Pickwick Papers, where a maker of meat pies attests that he can alter flavors readily even though the raw material input is unchanged, "make a weal a beef-steak or a beef-steak a kidney, or any one on 'em a mutton, at a minute's notice, just as the market changes and appetites wary." The raw material input was baked tabby cat.*

The reason for this is that the rising price for college rings will entice Welkin to produce more of these and less of its other kinds of rings simply because more *profit* will be earned by doing so.

Welkin's position may be shown in the following table of hypothetical data:

If the price per unit is:	Then the quantity of college rings the firm will supply in some time period (one year) will be:	
High	$50	Very high	1,000
Medium	$25	Medium	400
Low	$10	Low	100
Zero	0	Zero	0

This data can be plotted as was done with demand, with price on the vertical axis and quantity supplied on the horizontal axis. Points 1, 2, 3, and 4 on Figure 2–11 correspond to the figures in the table, and if we had more such data, and hence more such points on the diagram, they would appear to lie along a curve as shown. This is called a *supply curve*, labelled S.

This entire discussion of supply has been limited to one seller only, the Welkin Ring Company. The next step is to determine the supply in the whole market among all the sellers of a particular good. The technique is exactly the same as the

FIGURE 2–11

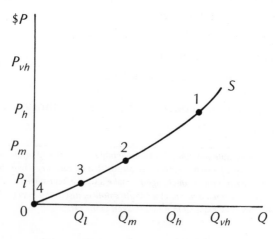

method used in finding total demand in a market. We simply add together, horizontally, all individual supply curves to find total or market supply.

In Figure 2–12 below, the left hand curve shows the supply curve of the Welkin Ring Company, the middle figure shows the supply curve of another supplier, the Niebelungen Ring Company, and the right-hand diagram shows the two added together.

At any price on the vertical axis, the quantity supplied to the two-firm market is equal to the horizontal distance over to the supply curve. See how S_{w+n} at a price of $50 is Welkin's 1000 plus Niebelungen's 750, which equals 1750; while at a price of $25, with $S_w = 400$ and $S_n = 500$, $S_{w+n} = 900$.

When discussing total supply note carefully that in addition to the six determinants of a single seller's supply presented earlier, one further determinant must now be considered. Total supply depends also on the number of sellers in the market. Obviously, the larger this number, the more supply curves to be added together, and the further to the right the total supply curve will be.

Do Supply Curves Always Slope Upward?

Just as we looked for exceptions to the downward slope of the demand curve, it is useful to look for exceptions to the rule that market supply curves slope upward from lower left to upper right. Actually, there are not likely to be many exceptions. For if one seller is, as seen earlier, tempted to shift his output to the good which rises in price, all other things being equal, this will be even more true when all potential sellers are considered. A sharp rise in college ring prices might lead any number of firms not hitherto making them to enter into their production. Any firm with experience in metal-working might

FIGURE 2–12

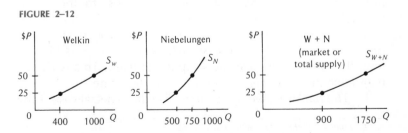

have a go, and for that matter, new firms could be formed just for the purpose of tapping the high profits expected because of the price rise.

However, three special cases among supply curves deserve mention: the horizontal curve, the vertical curve, and the "backward-bending" curve.

1. *The horizontal curve.* Under some circumstances, a higher price would not be needed to persuade firms to supply greater quantities of a particular good. Say production is profitable at a price of OP in Figure 2–13 for some easily repro-duceable item such as nails, pins, pencils, and so forth. It is logical to suggest that the firms producing this sort of product could increase their output considerably with little extra effort. A few more men, a few more machines of the type already being used, and yearly output could rise by many millions. Within wide limits, firms might stand ready to supply any quan-tity shown on the diagram at the old price of OP. The supply curve which mirrors this situation is a horizontal line.[14]

FIGURE 2–13

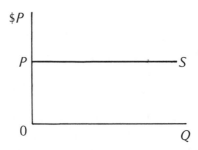

2. *The vertical curve.* The exact opposite is the case where the quantity supplied is fixed in amount no matter what the price. There are a myriad of possible examples, ranging from Botticelli paintings and Donatello sculptures, to the bread available in a city under seige or cut off by floods, to the amount of beer available in the town's only grocery store late on Saturday night. In each case, whether the price is high or low, the amount that can be supplied is fixed. This is shown diagrammatically in Figure 2–14, by a vertical line.[15]

3. *The backward-bending curve.* The last special case is the

---

[14] *Economists call this a "perfectly elastic" supply curve.*
[15] *This is called a "perfectly inelastic" supply curve.*

FIGURE 2-14

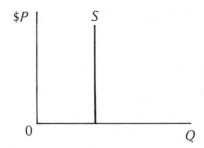

oddest in appearance (see Figure 2–15), and receives its name from its noticeable turn toward the upper left in the diagram. Backward-bending supply curves are a possible phenomenon in the market for labor. In an unpleasant occupation—mining, for example—workers may dislike their work so heartily that a rise in wages will cause them to work fewer hours. The individual miner may simply say to himself, at the new higher wages being paid I can afford to work fewer hours for the same total income. Above the arrow in Figure 2–15, this reasoning applies. Such behavior has been reported in several less developed countries where workers come from villages with the aim of earning a certain target income, after which they will return to their homes. It may also apply to recipients of social security who are limited to the total outside income they can earn without forfeiting their benefits (in 1974, $2,400).

What Information Does a Supply Curve Give?

As with demand curves, a supply curve can also depict many different economic events. Most obvious, it shows what occurs

FIGURE 2-15

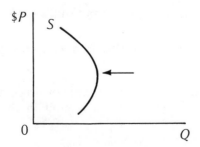

FIGURE 2–16

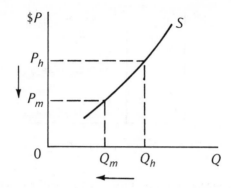

when, in a time period, price changes. In Figure 2–16, we see that a fall in price (with no alteration in any of the other determinants of supply) from OPh to OPm results in a decrease in the quantity supplied from OQh to OQm. This kind of movement is always called a *change in the quantity supplied*.

Like demand, the supply curve is a very pliant tool which can readily be adjusted to reflect changes in our underlying assumptions. Suppose for the moment that our dicta concerning constant costs, unaltered technology, or any of the several other assumptions behind the supply curve, are temporarily relaxed. In that case the supply curve itself may well move.

The supply curve for college rings is shown in Figure 2–17. Remember that this shows the relation between changes in price and changes in the quantity sellers will supply with all the others determinants held constant. But what if any one of the following should occur:

1. Costs of the factors of production decline.

2. The market price for wedding bands (substitutes in production) falls.

3. New technological advances result in more efficient ring-making machines.

4. The number of companies producing college rings is growing steadily.

The result will be a greater supply of rings, and is shown in Figure 2–18 as a rightward movement in the entire supply curve.

FIGURE 2–17

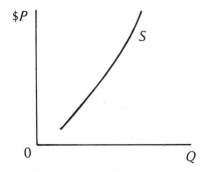

At a high price such as OP$_h$, lower labor costs or new technology will result in a greater supply. Sellers who previously were willing to market a quantity OQ$_m$ at a price of OP$_h$ will now be willing to sell OQ$_h$. Or at some lower price OP$_l$, sellers who formerly marketed OQ$_l$ are now persuaded to sell a higher quantity, OQ$_m$.

The outward (rightward) movement in the supply curve itself has taken place because of an alteration in one or more of the determinants of supply which had previously been held constant. This sort of movement will be termed a *change in supply*.

The events which would cause a decrease in supply should be readily apparent. For example, reversing the logic of points 1 through 4 above would have the effect of moving the supply curve inward (leftward), as in Figure 2–19.

FIGURE 2–18

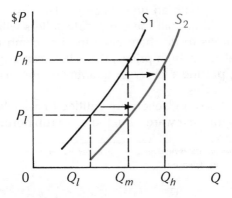

FIGURE 2–19

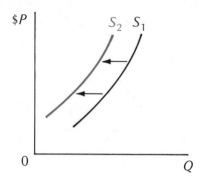

DEMAND AND SUPPLY TOGETHER

We have now analyzed the shape of both demand and supply curves in some detail. The conclusion is that under ordinary circumstances, demand curves slope downward from upper left to lower right, while supply curves slope upward from lower left to upper right. All this has been in preparation for seeing how prices are determined in a market system.

The first step is to put both the demand and the supply curves for a product on the same diagram. We will again choose a simple example and select for investigation the price of the tasty dates on sale at the local market in the lonely Saharan oasis town of El Golea.[16]

There is every reason to believe that the demand curve for these dates has the standard downward slope. At higher prices, the inhabitants will eat other foods; at lower prices, they will consume more dates. Similarly, the supply curve should be normal enough, with an upward slope. Low prices will mean that Hassan, Ali, and all the other date sellers will have more profitable things to do than make the hot climb up the date palms. At relatively high prices, the sellers can afford to climb all day long, putting a far larger quantity on the market. Figure 2–20 illustrates this.

In a market system, sellers are entitled to ask whatever price they want to for their wares. But there is a rub here: consumers

---

[16] *The author bought dates here once on a trans-Saharan auto trip, and so, unlikely as it seems, writes from experience.*

FIGURE 2–20

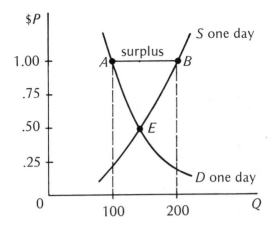

are not forced to buy at these prices. The diagram shows this vividly. Suppose that early on market day, Ali, Hassan, and their friends begin to stick price tags into their respective piles of dates, and the price they choose is $1.00 per lb.[17]

Although the sellers are completely free to try to sell at this price, the result is discouraging. They soon discover that though they stand ready to provide, say, 200 lbs. of dates at a $1.00 price (follow the vertical line down from point B on the supply curve), buyers find that price high and will only be willing to buy 100 lbs. (see point A).

The horizontal distance AB represents the 100 lbs. of dates which will go unsold at a price of $1.00. There is a surplus. Businessmen do not like to be stuck with unsold stocks of goods. No profit is being earned on them, and there is the problem of storage and spoilage which both represent costs. If they are to sell the stocks, the only reasonable solution is to cut the price to something below $1.00.

What would happen if a big cut is made, to 25¢ per lb.? In Figure 2–21 two results are apparent. At the new low price, the sellers are only willing to put 90 lbs. of dates on the market that day. Some of them would prefer to have a day off, or work in their vegetable garden, or whatever, rather than bother with

---

[17] Or rather its equivalent. El Golea is in Algeria, and so the correct measure would be Algerian Dinars per Kilogram.

FIGURE 2–21

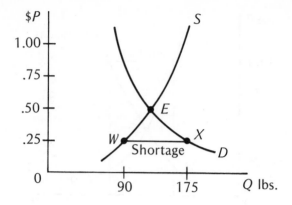

dates at that price. On the other hand, consumers are filled with joy, and flock to the market to buy at this economical rate. The quantity demanded in the diagram is 175 lbs., at 25¢ per lb. The result is likely to be distressing to buyers and sellers alike, for if that price level persists, there will be an obvious shortage of 85 lbs. Too little is on sale to satisfy all the people in the market who want to buy dates at their prevailing low price.

Something will have to happen. When it does, it is likely to take one or both of two forms. First, one of the sellers might raise his prices on the spot. Second, a dissatisfied buyer not able to buy the amount he desires may simply offer more money for an extra pound or two.

Another look at Figure 2–21 will show that *any* price above the intersection of the demand and supply curves (labelled "E" on the diagram) will result in the generation of an unsold surplus. The size of the surplus is the horizontal distance between the curves, as on Figure 2–22, where it can be small (FG) as at a price of 60¢, or large (HJ) as at $1.25. But in both cases market forces will be exerting pressure on sellers to cut their price. And the scenario is more convincing because any eccentric seller too lazy to worry about his surplus will surely lose all his sales (probably even to his relatives) if others cut their prices but he does not. There is always a pressure downward until there is no longer any excess supply of unsold output. The price level where no such surplus will be in evidence, as mentioned earlier, is marked E. Meanwhile, *any* price below E will have the converse effect of leading to an excess of quantity demanded over quantity supplied, that is, a shortage. As on

FIGURE 2-22

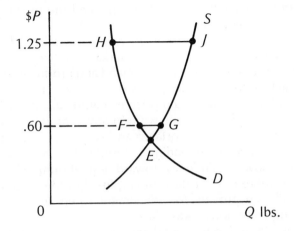

Figure 2-23 the magnitude of the shortage may be large (KL at a price of 10¢) or small (MN at a price of 40¢). But in both cases the deficiency will lead to an upward pressure on prices, and this tendency will disappear only when they have risen as far as E.

That price level marked E now can be seen to have a special significance. Only there, at a price of 50¢ per lb., is price high enough to avoid the shortage caused by an excess of demand, and low enough to escape the surplus that comes from excess

FIGURE 2-23

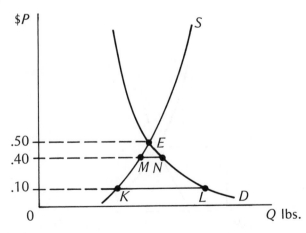

supply. E here stands for "equilibrium"—the only price where the quantity that sellers want to supply and the quantity that buyers want to consume are equal.

The concept of equilibrium price is a central pillar in the market system. Through this remarkable device, the two economic forces of consumers' demand and producers' supply so interact as to "clear the market." That is, the pressures which lead to an equilibrium price will automatically, without human command nor indeed without any conscious direction at all, tend to eliminate shortages and surpluses in a market.

This framework is exceedingly flexible. The last paragraph discussed how a tendency toward equilibrium will result whenever there is a shortage of surplus. But the same mechanism will also provide for adjustment when any change in underlying conditions takes place.

In Figure 2–24, the price of dates per lb. is shown in equilibrium at 50¢. However, what if a fundamental alteration occurs in the determinants of either demand or supply? Take demand first. What if a new oil strike raises the income of villagers, and also brings more people to the oasis? What if the younger generation of oasis-dwellers shows its independence by becoming heavy date consumers? Or perhaps the price of competing figs rises. In every case, the demand for dates will increase, possibly as pictured in Figure 2–25, where D_2 shows the higher demand. A new equilibrium price at a higher level is obvious (at OE_2, above OE_1). Rule: with standard-shaped curves, a rise in demand will raise the equilibrium price, and

FIGURE 2–24

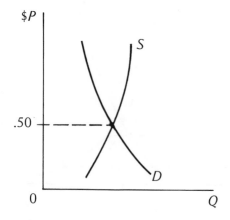

FIGURE 2-25

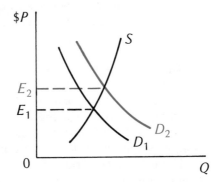

conversely, a fall in demand will lower equilibrium price. Remember, there is no guarantee that any seller will always charge just that new figure, although there is an economic pressure toward that position.

The mechanism is equally adept at handling changes in supply. Say a spell of perfect weather means more raw dates on the palm trees, or the cost of hiring boys to climb the trees falls, or new cleats speed the tree-top harvesting, and so on. These all represent an obvious way to increase supply, shown as a rightward movement in Figure 2-26. Such an increase causes a decline in the equilibrium price from OE_1 to OE_2. Rule: with standard-shaped curves, a rise in supply will mean a rightward movement of the curve and a decrease in the equilibrium

FIGURE 2-26

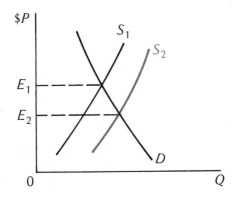

price, and conversely, a decrease in supply will mean a leftward movement of the curve and an increase in price.

Any underlying change in the building blocks of supply and demand will, therefore, result in a new equilibrium.[18]

Now pause a moment to reflect on the unique adaptability of this mechanism, as well as its universal application to anything marketable. It is this system that explains analytically why certain used British Guiana one-penny or Mauritius Island two-penny "Post Paid" stamps (each one at the end of the stamp collector's rainbow) can cost hundreds of thousands of dollars today (very low supply and intense demand from rich collectors), while a used 5¢ President Eisenhower stamp vintage 1965 costs less than 5¢ (enormous supply, limited demand.) Or why the water to clean the decks of a boat on Lake Michigan is free (enormous supply compared to demand), while the water at El Golea oasis is sold at a price (limited supply compared to demand). Or why a 1974 Cadillac costs more than a 1965 model but less than a 1920 Cadillac which commands a very high price among connoisseurs.

And for flexibility, note recent newspaper reports that Turkish peasants get about 25¢ per lb. for opium latex, which after processing in the laboratories of Marseilles is valued at around $5,000 per lb. of wholesale heroin. This same pound landed in New York may be worth $12,000 wholesale and out on the street perhaps $120,000 retail in unadulterated form. At every

---

[18] *Where the shape of either of the curves is abnormal, the effect on price will deviate from the rules above. Where the supply curve is horizontal (Figure 2–27) a change in demand leaves prices unaltered. Where supply is fixed (a vertical curve as in Figure 2–28) a change in demand affects price only, and not surprisingly cannot make a difference in the quantity supplied. Where the supply curve is backward-bending, an increase in demand will cut back the quantity supplied as price rises. Readers will find further unusual results if they consider changes in supply in a diagram where the demand curve is vertical or horizontal.*

FIGURE 2–27

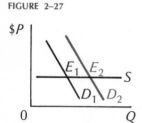

FIGURE 2–28

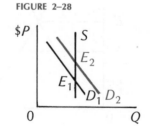

stage, supply and demand are working together to indicate a market price.

However, the really remarkable feature of the market mechanism does not lie in these exotic cases. It lies instead in the more worldly activities of millions of buyers and sellers, trading in millions of goods and services, bought and sold every day in the transactions which are the essence of modern economics. Whenever this market mechanism operates unimpaired, and whatever its faults otherwise, it is seen to be an automatic eliminator of shortages and surpluses; it does not need an army of bureaucrats to run it nor an iron law of feudalism.

Questions

1. What did the classical economists think determined prices? What error did they make?
2. What are the determinants of demand? Of supply?
3. What is the difference between a change in the quantities demanded and supplied, and changes in demand and supply?
4. What is the explanation for the unusual shapes exhibited by some demand and supply curves?
5. What is an equilibrium price? What causes the tendency toward equilibrium?

3.

GOVERNMENT INTERVENES IN THE MARKET

For political reasons governments occasionally feel the need to intervene in the operation of the market. Four such cases are (1) price controls and rationing, (2) maximum rent and interest (usury) legislation, (3) agricultural price supports, and (4) minimum wage laws. Our theory of supply and demand allows us to make some interesting predictions when the government adopts these policies.

PRICE CONTROLS AND RATIONING

In times of serious shortage, particularly in time of war, reduced supplies of food, fuel, and essential items work through the market mechanism to drive prices up. At such times, only those with high incomes will be able to afford the necessities, while most of the population suffers. Consider the high price of steak. Governments may respond to this by setting a fixed price at some low level which everybody can afford, say at OP_f in Figure 3–1 in place of the very high market price OP_h which thereafter becomes illegal. A glance at the diagram shows that a problem will result, however. At the legal maximum price OP_f, the amount producers will be willing to supply is limited to the low quantity OA, while consumers would like to purchase the much higher quantity OB at the government price. The distance AB represents the "excess demand" which makes itself felt as a shortage. In the week the author wrote this passage (in Istanbul, Turkey) a strange thing happened in the butcher shop where his wife always bought the family steak.

FIGURE 3–1

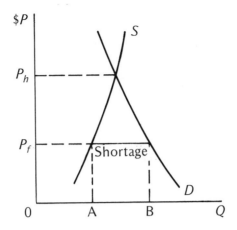

Suddenly on a Monday morning no steak was available. Nor was there any on Tuesday or Wednesday. Hurried questioning revealed that the police had begun to enforce price control regulations on meat, regulations which previously had gone unheeded. So, instead of getting steak your famished author got hamburger made from raw materials known only to Allah and the sulky butcher.

It is common where police surveillance is not continuous and where the force of public opinion does not compel conformity, for illegal "black market" sales to occur in this situation; indeed, on the next Thursday the butcher whispered that he would gladly sell us steak at a price of about 50 percent over the fixed level. Do not conclude that the black market price is necessarily the same as OP_h in Figure 3–1. Many sellers will fear police action or will suffer pangs of conscience so that supply for the black market will be restricted. Demand will be lower on the black market for the same reasons. The new supply and demand curves will intersect somewhere above OP_f, but the black market price could well be lower, higher, or by chance identical to the free market price. In Figure 3–2, D_{bm} and S_{bm} together give a black market price of OP_{bm}, slightly lower than OP_h.

If buyers and sellers do not want to participate in the black market, then when price controls are established below equilibrium, how will a seller distribute his supplies OA among his customers who want OB? Several methods are available. He

FIGURE 3–2

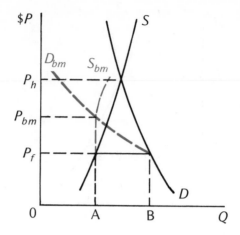

can sell his supplies on a first-come-first-served basis just as soon as he receives them. In Britain, use of this technique gave our language a new use for the word queue, for like the long braided hair of Chinese men, customers would have to stand in line for hours outside shops as they waited for supplies to arrive. However, this method is not only time consuming but unfair to those who must do without. Alternately the shop-keeper may allocate the scarce commodity himself, perhaps to friends and familiar customers. Presumably this method is the reason why in Istanbul Mrs. Hogendorn found no steak on sale for several days—not enough influence with the butcher.

To avoid this situation, governments may decide to establish a system of rationing. Ration books containing coupons for each good, say, one gallon of gasoline or one pound of meat, are issued to the general population. The quantity of coupons issued in the case of Figures 3–1 and 3–2 would be exactly equal to OA. The buyer will now need not only enough money to pay the price OP_f per unit, but a ration coupon as well. Demand is thus artificially restricted to no more than a quantity OA. The system was first implemented on a large scale in World War I, when it was used for particularly scarce products.

Rationing was rushed back into use at the start of World War II. However, growing money incomes earned by those em-ployed in defense industries, which could not be spent on rationed goods, led to what was known as "spreading the short-ages." Money not spent on rationed meat might be spent on unrationed fish, quickly causing sharp price rises for the latter.

To counter this, point rationing was invented by the Nazi Germans, whence it spread first to Great Britain and then to the US. Under point rationing, ration coupons of a certain point value would be issued, say, for clothing, and the consumer could choose among all the various sorts of clothes where to "spend" his points. It became a simple matter to curtail overall consumption. For instance, a 50 percent cut in clothing consumption could be achieved at any time by reducing the number of points distributed by half. In Britain during the worst days of World War II, some drastic examples of rationing included two pints of milk a week and one egg a month! In the US, ration coupons—red for meat and butter, blue for fruits and vegetables, etc.—are collector's items today.[1]

As this book was going to press it appeared likely that Americans would once again obtain some first-hand experience with rationing. The Arab oil boycott had so constricted supplies of gasoline and home heating oil that peacetime rationing was becoming a distinct possibility. One new twist among the several proposals being aired was a program of government control with a built-in device to curtail the black market. Black markets develop, as seen above, in response to the shortages which are created at the low official price. Some people will want a good such as gasoline so desperately that they are willing to break the law to obtain it. Why then not simply legalize the black market? Proposals calling for a legal "white market" envisage a fixed amount of gasoline being rationed to consumers by the normal coupon method. Anyone wanting more gasoline could then buy it from anyone wanting to sell at whatever the market will bring. The "white market" price would be determined as in Figure 3–2, with supply and demand giving an equilibrium above the official fixed price. The major advantage of this method would be to eliminate much of the large bureaucracy which must spring up to police the system when a white market is not permitted. The bureaucracy problem is bad enough even without black markets to worry about. In January, 1974, there was endless discussion of how coupons should be distributed if gasoline rationing were instituted: by number of automobiles, by number of licensed drivers, by family, and with or without consideration of those who commute long distances or travel by car for a living.

---

[1] On these stamps are portrayed various warlike pieces of equipment, bombers, tanks, and so forth, which were curiously old-fashioned even for the time and from their appearance would have fared ill on the battlefields of Europe.

In Europe, where the winter energy crisis of 1973–74 appeared to be even worse than in the US, rationing systems were in readiness by the Christmas season. Great Britain had already printed its supply of ration books and stamps, and unless the situation underwent rapid improvement, British control measures were expected imminently. Rationing, in short, appeared ready to jump from the economics textbooks to the front pages of the world's newspapers.

RENT MAXIMA AND ANTI-USURY LEGISLATION

Similar logic applies to government-imposed rent maxima and anti-usury ceilings on interest rates. Both may be useful social measures, but the economist is bound to point out pitfalls which are likely to surround legislation of this type. Note Figure 3–3. A government rent maximum anywhere above the equilibrium rent OR_e which would exist in the absence of government action would make no difference. However, a rent ceiling below equilibrium, as at OR_{max}, would tend to cause a shortage of rental housing equal to Q_1Q_2. At the low rent required by law, there is a greater quantity demanded than would be the case at equilibrium, while availability of rental housing is restricted by the artificially low return to landlords.

Two examples of rent control in operation are in New York

FIGURE 3–3

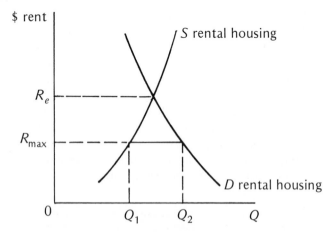

and London. New York has had rent control since 1943 (applying to about half of the city's housing units) and has traditionally been afflicted with a chronic housing shortage. City officials consider that housing conditions are in a state of emergency when vacancies are less than 5 percent of all housing, but figures below 2 percent have been common in New York for extended periods. In London, rent of so-called "council housing" introduced by the Labour government after World War II has been under continuous strict control, while other uncontrolled housing has undergone an unparalleled boom. The result is virtual no-vacancy conditions for council housing, with long lists of applicants, tiny turnover of tenants, and years of waiting for a controlled apartment.

Likewise, anti-usury laws[2] which set a maximum rate of interest on loans can have the effect of creating a shortage of funds for lending. Such laws are among the oldest in our economic heritage. "The most hated sort" of economic activity, says Aristotle, "is usury, . . . of all modes of getting wealth the most unnatural."[3] Christ said "And if ye lend to them of whom ye hope to receive, what thank have ye? For Sinners also lend to sinners, to receive as much again."[4] By the ninth century A.D. interest had been prohibited by the ecclesiastical authorities, and this stance was canon law of the Roman Catholic Church until 1917. Almost all states now prohibit interest rates over some maximum level. Such laws do have a predictable effect as shown in Figure 3–4. Assume the market rate of interest would have been Oi_e except for a usury law which makes the maximum permissible interest rate Oi_m. Here, the lower rate will stimulate demand for loans and simultaneously restrict the supply of funds for lending. A shortage equal to the amount Q_1Q_2 will develop, as some borrowers must go without loans at interest rate Oi_m. On many occasions in recent years, interest maxima have caused problems for home buyers seeking mortgages, and for students seeking bank loans to finance college tuition.[5] It is often argued that such shortages of loanable funds will cause prospective borrowers to turn to loan sharks.

---

[2] In the Middle Ages, the word usury meant any interest rate, while nowadays it means very high interest rates.

[3] Aristotle, Politics, Book 1, Chapter 10.

[4] Luke 6:34.

[5] Interest rates on mortgages rose sharply in mid–1973. Within weeks they had already bumped against the usury ceilings in New York, New Jersey, and Minnesota.

FIGURE 3–4

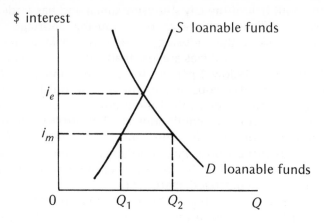

AGRICULTURAL PRICE SUPPORTS

Agricultural price supports, which date from the 1930s, are the opposite of rationing, rent controls, and anti-usury laws, in that government in this case interferes with the market to raise prices, not to lower them. Price supports in farming have their origins in the political influence of farmers in Congress (also true of the nine nations in the European Common Market). Arguing that farm incomes should be boosted by government action, Congress instituted three programs which had this result.

From World War II to the early 1960s the main program was government purchase of part of the crop to maintain prices at a high level. On Figure 3–5 note that the Department of Agriculture is determined to raise prices from equilibrium OP_e to a high level OP_h. This is easily (but expensively) done if the Department buys up a portion of the crop $AB = Q_1Q_2$ and holds it in storage. The excess of supply over demand which would have resulted at any price above OP_e is thereby eliminated, prices rise to OP_h, and the public cuts back its consumption of the product to OQ_1. Here the cost to consumers is the higher price they must pay plus the expense of keeping the commodity in storage. The surpluses, stored in giant bins all across the Midwest, were prominent features of the landscape until very recently, when a combination of foreign aid grain shipments to alleviate famine in India, and very large sales of grain to the USSR, reduced the surplus practically to nothing.

FIGURE 3-5

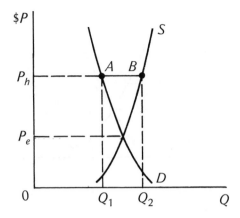

A second program, dating from the Eisenhower days, was the so-called "Soil Bank" wherein farmers were persuaded by cash payments to take arable land out of production. In economic terms, the expected result is clear: a reduction in the supply of agricultural commodities such as S_1 to S_2 on Figure 3-6. The resulting higher price OP_2 is expected to add to farmers' income.[6] The Soil Bank scheme has been troubled throughout its life, however, by farmers who put their worst land into the program, and who used the cash payments to buy fertilizer so as to raise output on their remaining acres. Where this took place, supply was not restricted after all and the program failed to achieve its aim.

From the Kennedy Administration until 1973, the basic policy followed was direct federal payments to farmers, which supported prices at high levels, combined with acreage restrictions on production. Direct payments, used most widely for wheat, feed grains, cotton, and wool, are illustrated in Figure 3-7. Here the market forces of supply and demand lead to production of a quantity OQ_1 at a price of OP_1. But to raise farmers' income to a higher level, a government "price support" or subsidy, here equal to the distance P_1P_s, is paid on every bushel or bale produced.

Two very serious charges must be leveled at the US farm program. The first concerns crop limitation. Right up to 1973,

---

[6] *The cost to consumers of farm products is thus the taxes levied to finance soil bank payments, and the higher price resulting as supply is reduced.*

FIGURE 3–6

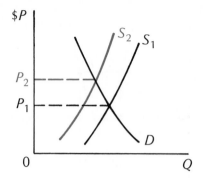

with food in short supply on a worldwide basis, and with meat in particular very high in price, the Department of Agriculture persisted in restricting farm output. This seemed sadly mistaken policy. One important reason beef is so expensive, leading to the housewives' meat boycott of 1973, was the limited output of corn and soybeans used to feed cattle. It is true that during that year only 8 million acres were held out of production, down from the all-time high of 35 million acres several years earlier. But 8 million acres is still about equal to the land area of Massachusetts and Connecticut combined!

In August 1973, a new agricultural bill was enacted into law, ending the controversial crop restriction program after nearly

FIGURE 3–7

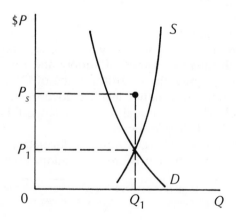

25 years of argument. The new bill is sometimes called the "Brannan Plan" because it was first proposed by President Truman's Secretary of Agriculture, Charles F. Brannan of Colorado. It establishes target price levels ($1.38 a bushel for corn, $2.05 for wheat) which correspond to the price P_s in Figure 3–7. Market prices will now be permitted to find the level set by supply and demand. Acreage restrictions and government purchases of part of the crop have no place in the new scheme. Subsidies will be paid only when prices fall below the target level. All in all, the bill is a great improvement on past policy, although it has come far too late to please the general public which bore the brunt of crop restriction when shopping for food.

The 1973 act does little to meet the second serious charge against our agricultural policy, which concerns the fairness of federal payments to farmers. Their ostensible justification has always been the low income of the average farm family—a third less than non-farm family income at the start of the 1970s. Subsidies are needed to rectify the deficiency, so it is said. In practice, however, things do not work this way. The benefits of government agricultural programs go overwhelmingly to wealthy farmers who rank far above the national average for income. Recent figures (1969) show that farms in the highest income categories, with sales of $20,000 per year and over, make up only 19 percent of the nation's farms but get a whopping 74 percent of all price support benefits. Meanwhile, the poorest categories of farms (sales less than $10,000 per year) make a large majority (64 percent) of all farms, but receive only 11 percent of total price supports.[7] It is clear that, whatever it does, the present US farm program is not designed to help poor farmers.

MINIMUM WAGE LAWS

Analagous to agricultural price supports are laws establishing a legal minimum wage which employers must pay. Most countries (but not all; for example, Denmark) have these laws. First in the US was the 25¢ per hour minimum wage established in 1938. As of 1973, the federal minimum is $1.60 per hour in

---

[7] See Charles Schultze, The Distribution of Farm Subsidies: Who Gets the Benefits (Washington: The Brookings Institution, 1971) for an excellent short survey.

occupations subject to the law. We can predict that where the established minimum is below the market wage actually being paid in an occupation (W_e in Figure 3–8), then the legislation will have no effect on wages. As with all the other cases discussed in this chapter, however, use of supply and demand curves allows us to predict some further effects of minimum wage laws. Workers who can find jobs at this rate (OQ_1 in the figure) will be paid the higher wage OW_m. But employment opportunities will decline at the same time from Q_2 to Q_1, as to some extent employers substitute other productive factors (machines, etc.) for the higher-priced labor. At wage OW_m, therefore, a quantity of labor Q_1Q_3 will be unemployed.

FIGURE 3–8

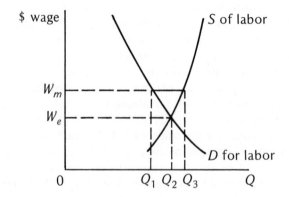

We can predict further that the unemployment Q_1Q_3 will be especially concentrated among teenage labor, minority groups, and the elderly, as these groups are often treated as marginal cases by employers, and are the first to be laid off when businessmen want to cut back on labor costs. There is not likely to be much support for a higher minimum wage among the 13 percent of teenage labor currently unemployed, nor among the much higher percentage of young blacks (30 percent) without jobs.[8]

In 1973 there was a strong push underway to raise the

---

[8] The Nixon Administration in 1973 was trying to establish a loophole permitting teenage workers to be paid 85 percent of the adult rate. Organized labor was fighting the proposal in Congress.

minimum wage. One bill which passed Congress established a new level of $2.20 (vetoed by President Nixon in September). George Meany and the AFL-CIO advocated a $2.50 wage floor to be reached in several steps. These proposals were generating much debate on the unemployment issue, with many economists calling instead for extended job training, retraining, information, and resettlement plans as more suitable alternatives to higher minimum wages.

In every case discussed in this chapter, government intervention in the market may well be justified on numerous grounds. But whenever such intervention is undertaken, both economic logic and the evidence of history predict that shortages will develop when prices are fixed below equilibrium, and that surpluses will occur when the fixed price is above equilibrium. There is an old saying, "you can't interfere with supply and demand," but this is quite wrong. You certainly can—but as we have seen, you must then bear the economic consequences when prices fail to reflect true wants and scarcities.

Questions

1. What do price controls, maximum rent and interest laws, agricultural price supports, and minimum wage laws have in common?
2. Why will rationing often be necessary under a system of price controls?
3. What costs are involved in agricultural price supports? Do they help poor farmers?
4. Who might be hurt by minimum wage laws? Why?

4.

PERFECT COMPETITION

In chapter 1 we saw that the price mechanism works as a signal-ling device, by which firms find the revenue they can earn from selling a product, the costs they will incur from hiring the fac-tors of production to make the product, and the profit that would be earned from its sale. With much reason, generations of economists believed that if these transactions are made under certain restricted circumstances called perfect (or pure) competition, the price system will work to maximize consumer satisfaction.

What is perfect competition? This common phrase is defined to mean that the number of sellers in the market is so large that no single one of them can influence the market price. Any seller takes the market price as given. He cannot sell more of his output by lowering the price, because by definition he can already sell any amount at the present market price. Further, any decision he makes to raise the price will result in a loss of all his sales, as buyers will simply fill their needs from compet-ing sellers. Recall the horizontal demand curve discussed ear-lier in Figure 2–5, where a single farmer was seen to be too small to affect the market for corn—an example of perfect competition in practice.

The inability of any single producer to alter the market price leads to three further requirements for perfect competition. First, the product sold must be identical among sellers, or "homogeneous." Otherwise, buyers who find such differ-ences would be willing to pay more for the preferred item. Second, entry into this industry by new firms must be easy. If it is not, then as sales grow and the original firms in the industry expand, the degree of competition may lessen substantially. Finally, knowledge of the market must be sufficiently wide-spread so that sellers cannot rely on lack of information about competing alternatives to boost their own prices.

In order to determine what quantity to produce, a firm

should determine the level of profit it can earn. Following the analysis of chapter 2, it will determine its total revenue at various prices and quantities, the total costs associated with these quantities, and the resulting total profit.[1]

TOTAL REVENUE

Let us begin with total revenue, which is a relatively simple matter. Under perfect competition, the price charged by a firm will not vary, whether sales are small or large. Any firm such as our old friend the Welkin Ring Company, should it be in a perfectly competitive industry, can calculate total revenue by multiplying the price charged times the quantity sold. Thus, if the competitive ring market dictates that the price will be $20 per ring, Mr. Welkin can calculate his total revenue from sales as in the following table:

Quantity of rings sold	Price of rings	Total revenue earned from sales
0	$20	$ 0
50	20	1,000
100	20	2,000
150	20	3,000
200	20	4,000
250	20	5,000

The information from the table can be neatly diagrammed as shown in Figure 4–1. The quantity sold by Welkin is measured along the horizontal axis (labelled Q). On the vertical axis are displayed various possible sales revenue in dollars. As we have seen, the link between the two is the price of the product, in this case $20. If 50 rings are sold for $20, the resulting total revenue of $1,000 can be shown on the graph at a point A, with coordinates of 50 and $1,000. Should 100 rings be sold at $20 each, TR is $2,000 as shown by point B. Similarly, C, D, and E show sales of 150, 200, and 250, respectively, with resulting TRs of $3,000, $4,000 and $5,000. A straight line through the points would show the total revenue at *any* quantity produced and is thus the line of total revenue (see Figure 4–2).[2]

---

[1] *TR − TC = TPr, as we discussed in chapter 1.*

[2] *Geometrically, the TR line has a positive upward slope of 20:1 which corresponds to our assumed price of $20 per unit.*

FIGURE 4–1

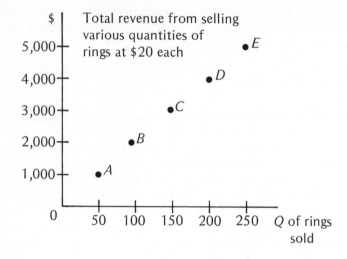

Total revenue from selling various quantities of rings at $20 each

Should market forces change the competitive price for rings for Welkin and all other producers, then of course total revenue would change also. A lower price of $15 per ring would give lower TR at any level of sales, as shown by TR2 on Figure 4–3. A higher price of $25 per ring would result in TR3, and so on.

No matter what the quantity sold or the price of the product, it is a simple matter for Welkin and for any other perfectly competitive firm to find the potential total revenue at any level of output.

FIGURE 4–2

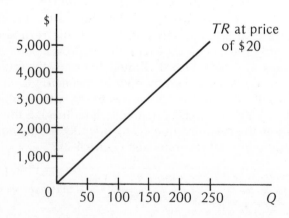

TR at price of $20

FIGURE 4–3

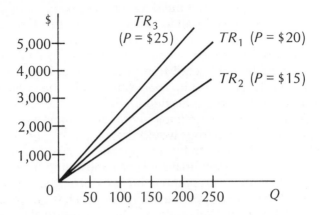

TOTAL COSTS

We now turn to a study of the costs of production, for without knowledge of costs it will be impossible to determine what is profitable.

There is a great difference between the concept of cost as usually understood by the ordinary citizen, and as understood by the economist. The central fact is that the economist measures more than the actual cash outlays of operations—and this is the key to correct measurement of total profits.

Take the Welkin Ring Company once again. There is no argument that the actual cash payments of the firm are an important element in costs. The accountant will usually find such costs easy to measure: wages and salaries for workers, outlays for raw materials and power, spending on buildings and machines, insurance, sales taxes, and the like. But consider this: what if Mr. Welkin spends a good many hours doing bookkeeping in the company office, but draws no salary for this because as the owner he takes the profits. The economist would say, "Aha, we have uncovered an additional cost." The time Mr. Welkin spends in the office is time he could have spent doing this kind of work for someone who would have paid him. Welkin is sacrificing this amount of income by doing unpaid work for himself. It is therefore legitimate to subtract from total revenue, as a cost, the implicit wage Welkin could have earned by working for pay elsewhere. This implicit wage is not an actual cash outlay, but in the term used by economists, it is an *opportunity cost*.

Similarly, there are other opportunity costs which can be identified. What about the buildings and land owned by Welkin? Could these not be rented to some other firm? If so, then we have uncovered another sacrifice by Welkin. The rent foregone by using its own buildings and land is also an opportunity cost, to be subtracted from total revenues in order to find the true level of profit. Then what about the capital invested in the firm? The funds tied up in the business could be put to some alternative use (most simply and almost risk-free in a savings account) where it would draw interest. The implicit interest on capital invested is an opportunity cost too. Finally there are the entrepreneurial services contributed by Welkin. We recall that the entrepreneur initiates projects, organizes them, and bears their risks, the return for which is the profit he receives. Obviously, Welkin could obtain a return for his entrepreneurial services in some other occupation. There must be some minimal amount of profit he would have to receive, or else he would liquidate the ring company. As with the other opportunity costs, this minimal amount of profit is properly a cost of the firm, and economists call it *normal profit*. Only after this necessary minimal amount of profit is subtracted from revenues do we have the correct figure for profit in the economist's sense. When so calculated, the resulting profit is named "abnormal" or "economic" profit.[3] Henceforth, whenever costs are referred to in this book they will include opportunity costs as well as actual cash outlays.

How do the costs of a firm behave in relation to the quantity produced by that firm? Here we must introduce time into our discussion, because costs will be very much dependent on whether we can increase the size of the factory (plant and equipment).

We can define a short-run period during which there is not enough time to alter the physical size and quantity of plant and equipment. The firm can, however, alter its output by more or less intensive use of its equipment, and by changing the size of its labor force, the input of fuel and raw materials, and so forth. Note that the short run is by no means the same amount of calendar time for different industries. A producer of cement may find it relatively easy to build a bigger plant and add equipment, so that the short run may be only a matter of a few

---

[3] *Other names sometimes encountered are "pure" and "real" profit.*

months. A shipping firm operating supertankers may find that its short-run period is a matter of several years, as ships take a long time to construct.

In the short run, there are two types of costs. As long as plant size cannot be changed, some costs must be incurred even if the plant produces nothing, and will remain the same even if large quantities of output are produced. These are the *fixed costs* of a firm. They include outlays on the buildings, for which rent must be paid, or if already owned, then the setting aside of funds to cover their depreciation and eventual replacement. Other fixed costs would be insurance, cost of maintenance and security, interest on outstanding loans, and the salaries of managerial personnel under long-term contract. Also do not forget the opportunity cost elements—the implicit return that could be earned by using the capital, land, and buildings else-where, plus the normal profit needed to retain entrepreneurial talent.

Recall that these short-run fixed costs will not vary with the quantity produced. A simple diagram of their behavior is shown in Figure 4-4. The dollar amount of fixed cost measured on the vertical axis from zero through low, moderate, and high levels, does not change with the firm's output shown on the horizontal axis, whether that output is zero or high in quantity.

There are other costs to consider, however. These are in-

FIGURE 4-4

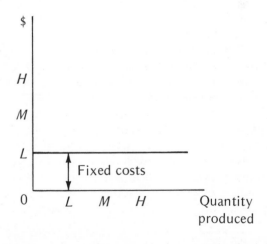

curred only because we produce, and are called the *variable costs* of the firm. Some obvious examples, already hinted at, are expenses for raw materials and power, wages for labor, and so forth. These costs will be zero at zero output, and they will clearly rise as output rises. Diagrammatically, they can be added atop fixed costs as shown in Figure 4–5, where we note that at zero output there are no variable costs. The line labelled TC shows the fixed costs plus the variable costs at any level of output, and thus represents the total cost of operations.[4]

FIGURE 4–5

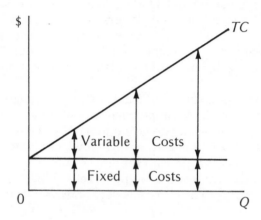

TC is shown here as a nice straight line, but actually the scenario is more complicated. A firm which starts up production is likely to find some economies developing in its variable costs as the quantity produced rises. Instead of a straight line, total costs will advance less rapidly than before over a certain stage of output, as seen in Figure 4–6. There are two main reasons for this: the division of labor, and economies in the use of plant and equipment.

The division of labor is a very old concept, first explored by Adam Smith in his *Wealth of Nations,* and is a powerful force for restricting the rise in total cost as output increases. The division of labor implies that each worker can be more efficient in doing one specific operation than in doing several. Using Smith's example of pin manufacturing, workers could make finished pins by themselves. But if these same workers spe-

---

[4] *Algebraically, TC = FC + VC.*

FIGURE 4–6

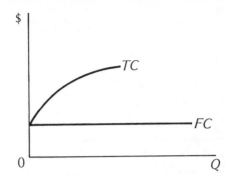

cialized in different tasks—some cutting the metal, some fashioning the heads, some the body and point—then more pins could be made in the same amount of time. Workers need no longer shift between tasks and tools and thus they save time. Repetition of an individual task would bring experience and proficiency.

Economies in the use of plant and equipment are a second explanation for the slowing rise in costs. Often such plant and equipment is indivisible. The Welkin Ring Company has to have a stamping machine of some minimum practical size and a trained man to run it.[5] At small quantities of output, the machine and the man tending it are operating far from full capacity. Their running speed is slow. But both machine and man are capable of running at a faster pace, more toward capacity output, with little increase in cost.

As production rises, however, there comes a point where total cost begins to rise more rapidly once again. Figure 4–7 shows this effect after output has reached a level such as OQ_1. The major reason for this is that production begins to overload the available plant and equipment. Recall that we are still speaking of the short run, when by definition these facilities cannot be altered in size.

We now have sufficient information to calculate an important further bit of information. It will be of great concern to Welkin, to any other firm, and to the consuming public generally to find the lowest cost of producing individual units of output. Where is this lowest cost per unit of output on our

---

[5] Part-time renting and hiring may allow a way out for the company, but it is often difficult to hire skilled people and specialized machines for short periods of time.

FIGURE 4–7

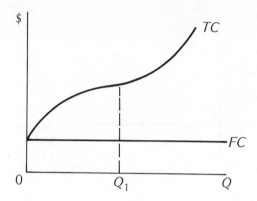

diagrams?[6] The calculation is simple. If the total cost of producing 50 rings is $2,000, then the cost per ring is $2,000/50 = $40. Should 100 rings cost $2,500, then cost per unit is $2,500/100 = $25. On Figure 4–8, note that point A corresponds

FIGURE 4–8

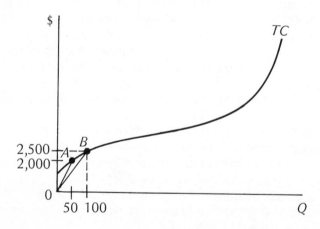

to TC = $2,000, Q = 50. The straight line from the origin O to A has a positive slope of $2,000/50, showing a cost per unit of $40. Point B reflects TC = $2,500, Q = 100, and the line OB has a slope of $2,500/100, a cost per unit of $25.

Note on Figure 4–9 that larger outputs C and D have even lower unit cost, as shown by the shallower slopes of OC and

---

[6] *Economists often call cost per unit "average cost" (AC), with algebraically AC = TC/Q.*

FIGURE 4–9

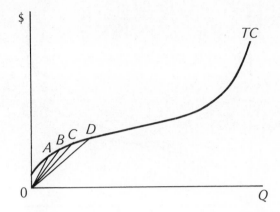

OD. The *lowest* per unit cost of all is shown by the line which touches TC with the lowest possible slope. Figure 4–10 shows that the unique position for this line, OM, is a tangency with the total cost curve. No other line can be drawn to TC with a lower slope, and output OQm is thus the level of production that minimizes unit costs. We have already seen that levels of production below OM give higher unit costs such as OA, OB, OC, and OD. Similarly, production levels above OQm will also be higher in unit cost (see Figure 4–11) as indicated by the steeper slopes of OE, OF, and OG.

Up to this point, the discussion has been limited to costs in the short run. As yet there has been no opportunity to expand

FIGURE 4–10

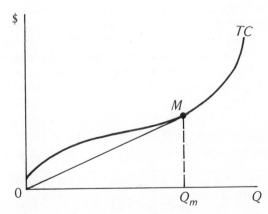

FIGURE 4–11

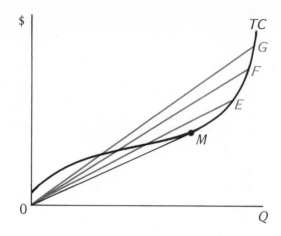

the size of the plant and equipment as production rises. In the long run, however, plant size is variable. Machines and structures too large for profitable operation can be sold off. Conversely, if expansion is limited by the constraints of plant size, this can be altered by building a new one. A familiar phrase in economics is that, in the long run, there are no fixed costs—all costs are variable because no outlays have to be permanent.

There are often economies involved in large scale operation, so that a new plant may bring lower unit costs than did the smaller plant being replaced. Such "increasing returns" or "economies of scale," as they are called, are made possible by the use of assembly-line techniques of mass production. The division of labor can be made ever more minute, with new individual tasks created to improve efficiency. Larger, more specialized, more complicated machinery can be installed and used at its most efficient speed of operation. From the first proven use of mass production in Eli Whitney's musket contract,[7] it flowered before the Civil War at the Colt arms works in Hartford, Connecticut, the Waltham watch factory in Massachusetts, and Cyrus McCormick's reaper works in Chicago. The maturity of mass production came at the River Rouge plant in Detroit where Henry Ford built the Model T; most modern manufacturing shares its heritage of mass pro-

---

[7] At Whitneyville, Connecticut, near New Haven, in 1798. Interchangability of parts was a Whitney innovation.

duction generating economies of scale as plant size expands.[8]

In addition, by-products can be utilized to reduce costs. For example, when refining petroleum on a small scale the very volatile gasses obtained might just as well be burned off into the atmosphere, while a large refinery can use these gasses to fuel its own processes, reducing energy costs significantly.

Finally, economies may result from large-scale purchases of raw materials and equipment. Suppliers may give price discounts on big orders of any input. It is also common to find that a building, ship, machine, etc., if doubled in size, costs less than twice as much to build.

These economies of scale mean that the unit costs for larger plants are reduced, as in Figure 4–12. Here TC_1 shows the cost curve for a small operation, TC_2 is the curve for a more sizeable plant, while TC_3 is larger yet. OM_1, OM_2, and OM_3 show the minimum unit cost declining for each plant size, with OM_3 the lowest of the lot.

FIGURE 4–12

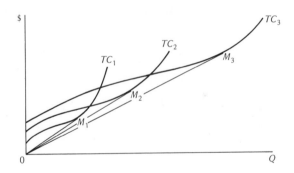

Economies of scale are not a permanent feature of expansion, however. In the long run, plant size may be pressed larger and larger in search of further savings in cost. But there seems to come a time, whatever the product produced, when the cost per unit begins to rise as scale increases. These "de-

---

[8] However, many observers believe that traditional assembly-line techniques will have to be altered in coming years to take account of increasing educational levels among young workers. The monotony and lack of responsibility have contributed to unrest, most notably at the Lordstown, Ohio, General Motors Plant. Redesigning the production line for "team work," pioneered by Saab in Sweden is gathering much support.

creasing returns" or "diseconomies of scale" are certainly not caused by any crowding in the factory, or by over-utilization of machines, as such cases can be corrected in the long run. Instead, the problem lies in the ever greater quantity produced by a firm which continually increases the demand for all the factors of production: labor, raw materials, and so on. There may come a time when these needs begin to raise prices on factor markets, meaning higher unit costs for very large plants.

Some economists also contend that diseconomies are due to management and supervisory problems which get progressively worse as scale expands. Extremely large plants will need a complex managerial staff organized on military lines. The delegation of authority may be so diffuse, decision-making through committees so complicated, that efficiency suffers and costs rise. Strictly, this cannot be the cause of diseconomies if we stick to our assumption that all factors, including high quality entrepreneurial ability, are available for hiring as needed. However, it is realistic to think that the human ability needed to run a gigantic concern efficiently is not common.

These diseconomies, when they set in, will appear as in Figure 4–13, where cost curve TC_3 is seen to have minimum unit cost (OM_3) while larger plants with cost curves TC_4 and TC_5 suffer from higher unit costs OM_4 and OM_5.

FIGURE 4–13

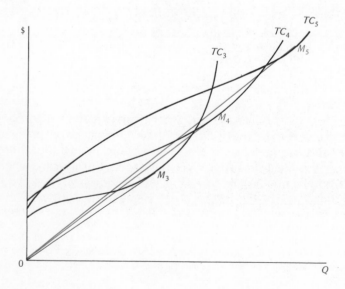

In some industries, economies of scale are realized over a very wide range of output. Motor vehicles and the milling of metals are perhaps the best examples.[9] In other industries, diseconomies set in rapidly, as in retail stores which generally find it inefficient to stock too many classes of goods (say fresh food, hardware, books, and clothing) under the same roof.

WHAT QUANTITY WILL BE SUPPLIED?

We now have enough information about our firm to discuss *what quantity of output it will choose to supply.* Assume for the moment that our firm is perfectly competitive. Given some market price for its product, it can thus calculate its prospective total revenues for any level of output. Our firm will also have an estimate of its costs. We are now familiar with both the line showing TR and the curve of costs TC.

These curves are what the firm will use to determine where profits are maximized. This is done first by recalling the rule that TR − TC = TPr, and then by *superimposing* the TR line for the going market price atop the firm's own curve of total cost. This is done in Figure 4–14, where TR is drawn on the assumption of a $25 market price for rings, while TC shows the short-run costs for our present plant. There is no need to put numbers along the axes to realize that this diagram has great significance for the company's production decisions.

What if it decides to produce only the fairly small quantity of rings OQ1? It is clear that at OQ1 total cost actually exceeds total revenue, so that the firm is making a net *loss* equal to the vertical distance AB. What about a higher level of output OQ2? At this level costs and revenues are exactly equal, and the company is just breaking even. This situation is duplicated at output level OQ4. Points W and X are called a company's *break-even* points. There will ordinarily be two break-even points: one is where economies of scale just begin to make production profitable (W) and the other at the much higher output level where diseconomies of scale begin to make production unprofitable once again (X). Recall, however, that "breaking even" in this context still means that a normal profit

---

[9] As we shall see, this is a crucial reason why perfect competition is not likely in these industries.

FIGURE 4–14

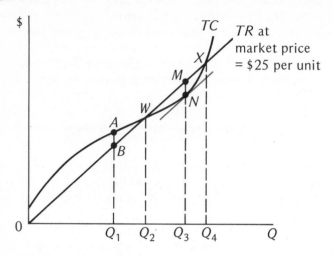

(already included in the cost curve) is being earned, allowing the firm to remain in operation.

Anywhere between output levels Q_2 and Q_4, TR exceeds TC so that an abnormal profit is being earned. Of most interest to the firm, however, will be that output which *maximizes* profit. This is clearly at the point where the vertical distance by which TR exceeds TC is the greatest, in this case at output OQ_3. Here the total profit is equal to MN, and no more lengthy vertical line can be fitted in the profit area between the break-even points W and X. In short, if this firm wishes to maximize its profits, given that the price of the product it sells is some fixed level (here $25), then it will produce a quantity of output equal to OQ_3.

There is a very neat rule of geometry which allows us to detect at a glance where this distance between TR and TC is greatest. Note that below N, TC is bending away from TR and the distance between the two is increasing as output expands toward N. Anywhere above N, TC is bending toward TR and the gap is closing as output expands. At N, the gap showing profit must be largest because TC has ended its trend away from TR but not yet started back toward it. At that point the slope of TC shown by a tangent line in red and the slope of TR are the same. In like manner, when other examples of cost and revenue are used in this book, the point of maximum profit can always be found quickly by discovering where TC and TR have the same slope. In future diagrams, a tangent line in red is the guarantee that we have picked the point of maximum profit accurately.[10]

In finding profit, we must now recall the distinction made earlier between the short run when plant size is fixed, and the long run when time is available to alter the scale of operations if desired.

FIGURE 4–15

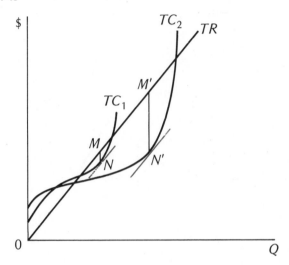

The plant size with the cost curve TC in Figure 4–7 may not be the plant of optimum scale. A larger plant might result in economies of scale, with a correspondingly lower cost per unit.[11] The economic motivation to build such a plant is shown in Figure 4–15. Given the same market price, and hence TR curve, the profits MN earned in the small-size plant TC_1 are much overshadowed by the bigger profit M'N' which occurs if the larger scale plant with cost curve TC_2 is built.

---

[10] *Economists call the numerical value of these slopes "marginal cost" and "marginal revenue." Most textbooks discuss profit maximization by developing these two marginal concepts at much greater length. However, this involves complications which, fascinating and useful as they may be, can be avoided by the presentation made above. A short discussion of "the marginal approach" is contained in the appendix to this chapter.*

[11] *Remember that a line from the origin O drawn tangent to a TC curve shows the minimum cost per unit (or average cost) of production.*

FIGURE 4–16

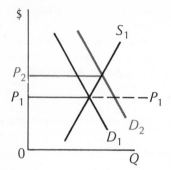

FIGURE 4–17

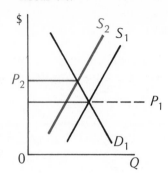

FIGURE 4–18

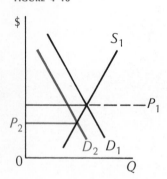

FIGURE 4–19

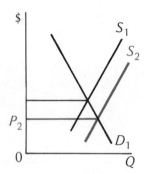

Thus these firms are not only maximizing the profit from their present plant, but also expanding to capture the even greater reward when economies of scale are realized.

The mechanism developed is, like market supply and demand, very flexible. To demonstrate, let us ask what the reaction of the competitive firm will be if the market price of its product changes. This could happen if there are variations in the overall demand for rings,[12] or if supply conditions alter.[13] Figures 4–16 and 4–17 show that such changes in market conditions may raise the price, while Figures 4–18 and 4–19 show a lower price.

The effect on the firm will be felt at once, because whatever

[12] *Due to buyers' greater desire to have one, or higher income, etc. (See chapter 2.)*
[13] *More sellers, cheaper labor, new techniques, etc. (See chapter 2.)*

the quantity of output sold, total revenue received will assuredly be different once the market price has changed. We will deal first with the case of a higher market price, say $30 per ring. With prices higher, total revenue must obviously be higher at any output level. Thus in place of the TR curve of Figure 4–14, we have the steeper curve TR2 of Figure 4–20.

The company will maximize its profits at this price by producing the greater quantity OQ1 (up from OQ), and total profits M'N' are clearly greater than the MN earned at the old $25 price. (Of course, common sense leads to expect that a higher price, with other things equal, will result in a higher total profit.)

The example can be reversed to find the effect of a price reduction, say to $20 per unit. Here a flatter TR line (TR3 in Figure 4–21) will result in a smaller quantity produced, OQ2, as the company alters output so as once again to maximize its profits M"N".

To summarize briefly, then: given its cost curve, a competitive firm which finds the price it receives rising or falling, will adjust its output so as to maximize its profits.

FIGURE 4–20

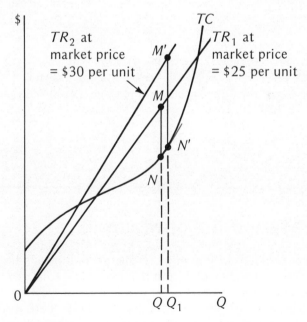

FIGURE 4–21

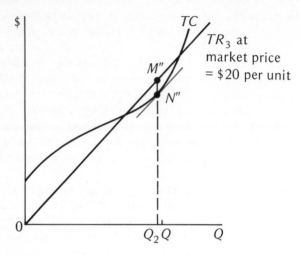

Questions

1. What is perfect competition?
2. What are opportunity costs? Are they included in the cost curve? Why is the total cost curve of a perfectly competitive firm shaped as it is?
3. How does a perfectly competitive firm decide what quantity to produce?

APPENDIX
The Marginal Approach

A central problem in the study of microeconomics is how to locate exactly the level of output that maximizes total profit. In this chapter we found that point with curves of total cost and total revenue as in Figure 4–22. Where TC and TR are furthest apart (MN at output level OQ), profits are at a maximum.

FIGURE 4–22

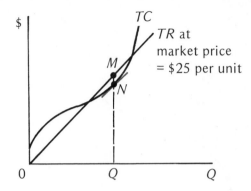

Geometrically, we explained that this greatest spread will occur where TR and TC have the same slope. In this way, we have implicitly used in simplified form the marginal approach, a fixture of economic theory for generations. Marginal concepts appear in more advanced microeconomic textbooks; this appendix will introduce, explain, and relate such concepts to the discussion in this chapter.

Take first the marginal approach to revenue. We have seen how total revenue climbs as output increases. However, it is also of interest to discover how much revenue is added by selling just *one* more unit of output. (In our example, this is seen to be $25.) The $25 may be called the "marginal revenue" (MR), that is, the additional revenue obtained from selling one more unit. Marginal revenue can be found easily on the diagram, because any time output is increased by one unit, total revenue rises by $25. The constant 25:1 upward slope of TR shows a constant marginal revenue of $25.

The marginal concept can also be applied to cost. Let us define marginal cost (MC) as the additional cost of producing just one more unit. On Figure 4–23, we see that total cost rises ever less rapidly with every unit increase in output up to OQ_1. Hence the marginal cost of each additional unit must be falling. In geometry, a tangent line to TC shows this visually. The tangent at A is steeper than at B, which is in turn steeper than the tangent at C, showing a steady decline in marginal cost down to a minimum at D. However, above output OQ_1 total cost begins to rise ever more rapidly. Hence marginal cost must also be increasing, as is verified by the ever steeper tangent lines at E, F, and G.

FIGURE 4–23

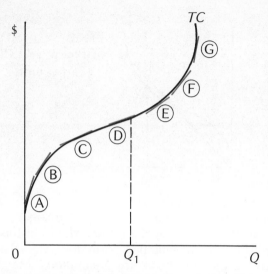

The importance of all this lies in the relation between marginal cost and marginal revenue at the output level chosen by the firm. Consider what it means for profits if the firm chooses to produce the quantity OQ_2 in Figure 4–24. At OQ_2 the marginal cost of the very last unit produced is much greater than the marginal revenue earned from selling it. ($25 is the marginal revenue in this case, but the marginal cost is about twice as much, shown by the steep slope of the red tangent to TC.) This means that the firm would increase its total profit by *not producing* this last unit. Conversely, at an output level OQ_3, the marginal revenue from producing the last unit ($25) is seen to be about double the marginal cost of that unit, shown by the shallow slope of the red tangent line. Whenever MR is greater than MC on the last unit produced, total profit can be increased by raising the level of total output.

The general rule enunciated in most textbooks can be summarized as follows. When MC is greater than MR, output should be reduced because profits are being sacrificed. When MR is greater than MC, output should be increased to raise profit. When MC is equal to MR, profits have been maximized and neither an increase nor a decrease in output will improve the profit position. Notice that this profit maximizing rule, MC = MR, is adhered to fully in Figure 4–24. At output level OQ_1, where profits MN are at a maximum, the slope of TR is the same as the slope of TC shown by the red tangent line.

FIGURE 4–24

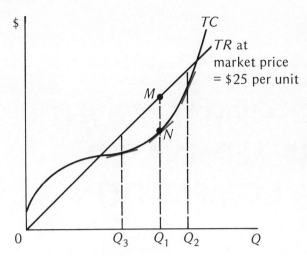

Marginal cost and marginal revenue, represented by the two equal slopes, are thus equal.

Throughout the remainder of the book, this marginal approach is used implicitly whenever we search for the point of profit maximization.

Question

1. How is the marginal approach used to give a rule for profit maximization?

5.

HOW ABNORMAL PROFITS ARE ELIMINATED BY COMPETITION

The profits discussed in the last chapter are, we have seen, abnormal profits; they are extra in the sense that a return just sufficient to keep the company in business is already included as a cost in the TC curve.[1] Thus these profits are pure gravy. Entrepreneurs looking for ways to earn higher incomes in a competitive economy will be strongly attracted to any industry earning abnormal profit.

As long as entry into the industry is easy (a requirement of pure competition, as seen earlier), many new firms are likely to set themselves up as competitors to cash in on the high rewards. For example, only a few years ago one company came up with the idea for snowmobiles; now the winter is shattered by the makes of several dozen companies, all spurred by profit to enter a profitable field.

Now note what this means, both in the market as a whole and for any single firm. For the market as a whole, the entry of many new firms will move the supply curve to the right from S_1 to S_2 as seen in Figure 5–1. The price level will be forced down, in this case by 25 percent from OP_1 to OP_2. The repercussions of the fall in price will be important for our single firm. Whereas at a market price of OP_1 it formerly garnered extra profits of MN (see Figure 5–2), the new lower price of OP_2 will

---

[1] See p. 56.

FIGURE 5–1

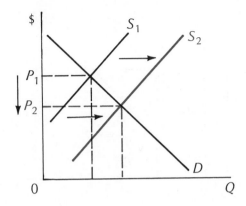

cut its profit level back to M'N', which is now the best that can be done.[2]

Even so, M'N' remains a healthy sum when viewed in the light that it is abnormal—it is more than needed to keep firms in the business. There is *still* an incentive for profit-seeking entrepreneurs to enter the industry, still a tendency for the supply curve to be pushed rightward, still an expectation of a decline in market price (see Figure 5–3). But this last event will have ominous implications for any single firm. The decline in market price from OP_2 to OP_3 (another 25 percent) will push

FIGURE 5–2

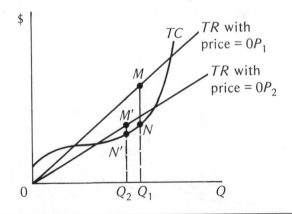

[2] *In the first case, profit MN is maximized at an output level OQ_1. In the second the greatest profit M'N' comes at output OQ_2.*

FIGURE 5–3

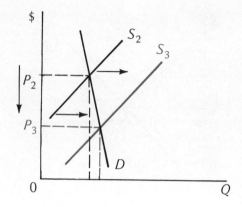

the curve of total revenue down even further to TR₃ in Figure
5–4. Now the curve for total costs lies everywhere above total
revenue. A profit cannot be made at any level of output; the
best that can be done is to minimize losses (KL) at an output
level OQ₃, where TR comes closest to TC.

In short, the excess of new competition means that individual firms are now incurring losses. The price OP₃ is just not
high enough to secure even that minimal return which will
keep firms in the industry. It is not difficult to predict the consequences: the weakest firms, or the ones whose entrepreneurs most quickly perceive other opportunities, will *leave*
the business.

Once more the supply curve shifts, but this time as firms

FIGURE 5–4

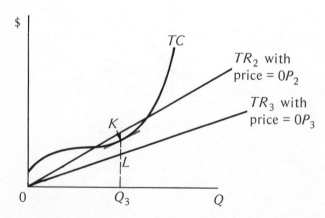

FIGURE 5–5

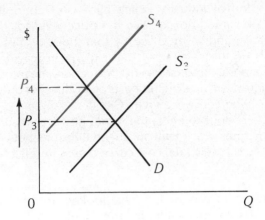

leave it moves leftward (Figure 5–5). Once again the market price changes, moving upward to OP₄. What if OP₄ is the price which would allow the total revenue line *just to touch* the total cost curve (Figure 5–6)? This would mean that although all extra profit has been competed away, the firm is not incurring losses because a return large enough to keep the firm operating is included as a cost in TC. Such a position is especially impor-tant, for only here is there no economic incentive for firms to enter or to leave the industry. Reaction and adjustment are no longer necessary. At a price OP₄, we can say that the industry and its firms are in a state of long-run equilibrium.

One complication must be dealt with. Thus far the competi-

FIGURE 5–6

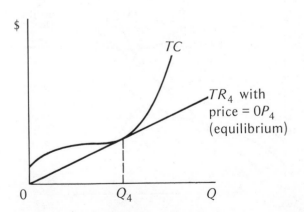

tive expansion of industry which eliminates abnormal profit has been presumed not to raise the price level for the labor, raw materials, and so on, used by that industry. But this may not always be the case. Industrial expansion may well cause shortages among these factors of production, meaning that any individual firm will face higher costs at any level of output (as in Figure 5–7) where TC_2 is above TC_1.

The logic of adjustment is the same, however, and as in our earlier examples will result in an equilibrium between total revenue and the new total cost curve drawn to reflect changed factor prices.

Generations of economists have looked on this framework as very desirable for society. It is not hard to see why:

1. The system reacts rapidly to the changing wants of consumers and to changing levels of cost. Desire for a good increases, thus raising both its price and the resulting profit accruing to the manufacturer. Higher profits attract more firms, with the consequence that more of the good is produced. It is hard to imagine other economic systems—for example, a Soviet-style central command economy—reacting so quickly either to consumer tastes or to costs.

2. The system works to minimize costs of production. Because of competition, abnormal profits will be eliminated.

FIGURE 5–7

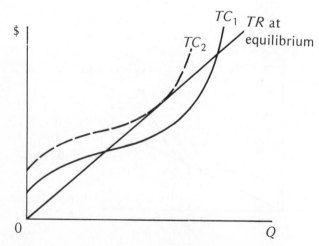

Firms that do not reduce unit costs to their lowest feasible level must thus incur losses. This is true of both the short run and the long run. In the long run, firms which do not take advantage of economies of scale in constructing their plant will find themselves losing their sales to firms who do, and can therefore charge the consumer a lower price. The most efficient cost cutting techniques must be adopted by all firms that want to survive under perfect competition.

3. The tendency for all profit (except normal profit) to be competed away means that the distribution of income in society is more equal than it otherwise would be. Artificially high profits cannot be the source of great personal wealth, and family dynasties formed from corporate ownership will be far less likely.

4. The minimization of unit cost and the elimination of abnormal profit both mean that the consumer will be charged the lowest price for the product consistent with the firm's survival.

This concurrence of highly favorable results explains the enthusiasm generated over the years by the theory of perfect competition. However, as we shall see in the next section, the market system is seldom perfectly competitive.

Questions

1. How does perfect competition work to eliminate abnormal profits?
2. What are the reasons for thinking that perfect competition is desirable for society?

II.

HOW THE MARKET SYSTEM CAN FAIL TO GIVE THE ADVANTAGES PREDICTED BY PERFECT COMPETITION

6.

PARADISE LOST, PART ONE: When Firms Have Control Over Price

We have seen that the perfectly competitive firm loses all sales if it raises its prices over the market price, and never feels the need to cut its price below market levels since it can sell all it produces at that figure. But there are many situations in which perfect competition cannot hold, so that a firm may gain a degree of control over the price it charges.[1] Let us examine several of these situations.

1.   One such case, perhaps the most important way a firm can obtain control over price, involves economies of scale. What if scale economies are so important that unit costs are quite high for limited output but decline significantly for increased output? This result, not infrequent in large mass-production industries, means that unit costs are relatively low only at some very large quantity of output. (See how unit costs in Figure 6–1 fall steadily, from the steep cost shown by OA at output level OQ_1, through OB at OQ_2, OC at OQ_3, and finally to the minimum unit cost shown by the shallow slope of OM at output OQ_L.)

But what if demand for this product is such that if the one firm was the *only seller*, it would earn the total revenue TR in Figure 6–2?[2] So far so good: the firm can obviously make a

---

[1] *When such control is present, economists speak of "imperfections" in the market.*

[2] *For a technical reason explained earlier, the straight line of TR must be made into a curve for strict accuracy in this example. But the theory is unchanged, and the conclusion is the same.*

FIGURE 6–1

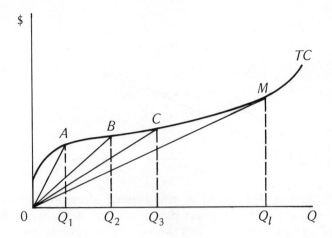

maximum profit equal to the distance XY if it produces the large quantity OQL. Now assume that *another* firm enters this industry and takes half of the sales, so that each one produces just half what it would have with only one firm present. (See OQ½ in Figure 6–3.) The important fact is that no profit can be made by *either* firm, because TR is far below TC at the smaller level of output. In short, one firm can exist profitably in this industry but two cannot. The weakest firm will presumably be driven out of existence.

The same situation exists when the cost curve is more normal (no particularly great scale economies) but market demand is

FIGURE 6–2

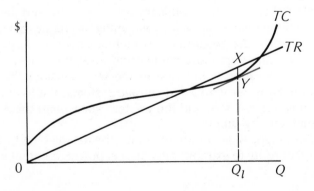

FIGURE 6–3

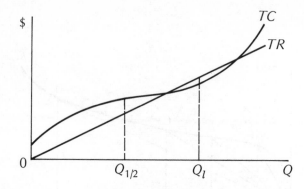

quite limited. For example, the general store in Caratunk, Maine, has potential market power for no other reason than that Caratunk cannot support two general stores, and there are no competing stores for many miles.

2. When government recognizes that very large economies of scale exist, as in the case discussed above, it may eliminate competition by granting a *public utility franchise* to a single company. In return for some state regulation of rates, the public utility is given a guarantee that no rival can enter that field. The state usually resorts to this system when the duplication of expensive capital facilities would be very wasteful. Imagine the expense and ugliness if two or more telephone companies strung wires on separately owned telephone poles in the same community. Imagine the inconvenience for families and firms who would have to pay for two or more phones. (In fact, in the early history of telephones in America this was the situation, and it has remained that way in a few foreign cities. Mexico City is a well-known case.)

Other examples of public utilities include water, electricity, and natural gas systems, public transport systems, and the like. Although the ownership of a public utility ordinarily remains in private hands, the government sometimes owns and operates the utility. Although more common in foreign countries, government operation is not rare in the US. Consider the post office, most water works and sewage systems, the hydroelectric dams of the T.V.A. and the western states, and the Alaska Railroad, among others.

Another type of government grant—the patent—has been an important route to extraordinary market power. A patent under

US law gives the holder exclusive rights to his invention for 17 years, and is non-renewable. Intended to reward and promote invention, patent legislation has led to market control by a single firm in several industries—the Eastman patents in photography, the Edison patents in light bulbs, the Bell patents in telephones, and the famous air-tight control of the shoe industry by the United Shoe Machinery Company are all cases from an earlier era. Note the misleading figure of 17 years in this context: a company that continues research on its basic invention may develop many patentable improvements and thus prolong its market hegemony many years after the original patents have expired. More recent patents in such fields as computers (IBM) and photocopying (Xerox) have been the base on which new industrial empires have been built.

A final class of government grants which discourage competition are tariffs and quotas. These policy tools keep foreign firms from competing on the same terms as domestic firms. If market power can be acquired, a stiff tariff or quota will help to ensure that it can be kept, at least where foreign firms are concerned.

3. Market control can come via a remarkably talented entrepreneur, who through his insights and vision, use of new techniques and new methods of organization, gains preeminence in his field. Henry Ford's rise to greatness is the most obvious example. Where ten years earlier there had been several hundred manufacturers of motor cars in the US, by the early 1920s Ford was selling more cars than all other competitors put together. Of course, continuation of this kind of market power depends on the grooming of talented successors—not always easy, as those who remember the Edsel can attest.

4. Sometimes a lucky or farsighted few gain control of some essential resource which gives market power. The sheik of some sandy Arab emirate and the Texas oilman have at least one thing in common: they did not put the oil there, but they own it now, and with oil as scarce as it is, competition declines. In any list of well-known examples such as radium, nickel, helium, and sulphur, the case of diamonds stands out. The DeBeers diamond concern in the Union of South Africa controls most of the world's high quality diamond supply and profits enormously thereby.

5. Entrepreneurs may find that the initial costs of becoming

established are so high that it is difficult to enter a business. Where large buildings, expensive machines, or extensive land-holdings are needed, even if the undertaking is guaranteed to be especially profitable, the number of competitors is likely to be small. This would not be important if entrepreneurs could be assured of access to bank loans, or easy sale of shares. But an unknown entrepreneur may be turned away by banks because of insufficient security, and his very inexperience may make his stock unsellable. No matter how promising his project, he cannot enter an expensive field on a shoestring.

Sometimes established firms may make entry more costly for newcomers. One tactic, usually illegal nowadays under the antitrust laws, is *selective price cutting*. At the turn of the century, a favorite device of John D. Rockefeller's Standard Oil Company was local price reductions which would force smaller competing oil refineries to merge with Standard or to leave the field altogether. The railroad rate wars of the late nineteenth and early twentieth centuries were an example of cutting charges to inflict higher costs on a potential competitor. A famous war in 1885 between Commodore Vanderbilt and the Pennsylvania Railroad resulted in Vanderbilt starting a new line (the South Pennsylvania RR) with many tunnels between Pittsburgh and Harrisburg. The rate war ended with a truce, the new line was abandoned, but you can see it today because its tunnels were purchased, cleaned out, and used for the Pennsylvania Turnpike. Most dramatic of all rate wars was in India, in 1946, when the India State Railways actually paid shippers to use their line.

More ordinary, but legal and quite effective, is the use of so-called *exclusive dealerships*. It is expensive enough to produce a new make of car. But that expense is boosted greatly because of the need to maintain a nationwide organization of exclusive dealers. A Ford salesman cannot sell you a Chevrolet, and that cost element helps explain why no new US auto maker has successfully entered the market since World War II.[3] Foreign auto makers face the same problem, and to break into the market a company must have either huge capital resources (as do Volkswagen, Fiat, and Toyota) with which to set up its initial dealerships, or it must depend on prestige so that customers will drive many miles to a dealer (such as Rolls-Royce, Jaguar, Mercedes, and Peugeot).

---

[3] *The last to try was Kaiser-Frazer, which gave up in 1953.*

Finally, any industry where advertising is important automatically imposes a higher cost requirement on new entrants. Cigarettes are a well-known example, with brand names so familiar to the smoking public that new brands must advertise on a princely scale to gain attention. Here too the high cost for newcomers can lead to market power for firms already established.

THE SPECIAL CASE OF MONOPOLY

"Market control" as used in the past few pages is a variable term. A firm can have only slight influence in its market, or it can have quite a lot, or it can be the only seller. The latter case we call *monopoly*, from the Greek words *monos polein*, or single seller. In today's economy, unregulated monopoly is very rare.[4] But the theory of monopoly behavior is nonetheless useful, because it is relatively simple and because many of its conclusions can be used to explain more common forms of business behavior.

A monopoly differs from a perfectly competitive firm in one critical way: its production decisions will affect the market. Assume that the Welkin Ring Company has a monopoly over the sale of college rings. Back in its competitive days, it dared not raise its price above what other sellers were charging, for then all sales would be lost to those selfsame competitors. But now the case is different. If Welkin raises its price, some people will indeed cease to buy rings, but others will be willing to pay the higher charge. Welkin is now the only firm in the industry, and thus the demand for its product is the demand curve for the entire market—which, as we have seen earlier, is ordinarily downward sloping. As Figure 6–4 shows, Welkin can produce various quantities of output, but each change will alter the price that can be charged. If OQ_1 is produced, then Welkin will charge a price OP_1.[5] However, if it raises its output to OQ_2, it "spoils" the price. To sell this larger quantity the firm will have to reduce its price (to OP_2 on the diagram).

---

[4] *Virtual monopolies were enjoyed for many years by Alcoa in aluminum, the International Nickel Company, the National Cash Register Company, and the United Shoe Machinery Company, among others.*

[5] *Other prices could be charged, but in every case except the one shown, the firm would end up with either shortages or surpluses.*

FIGURE 6–4

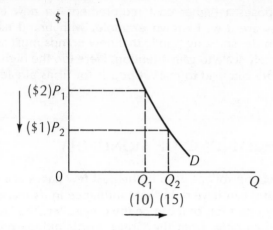

Right here the monopoly firm sees a problem. The fall in price may be so great that, even when multiplied by the higher quantity produced to find total revenue earned, TR may actually fall. This is clearly the case in Figure 6–4. The first quantity produced (10) when multiplied by its sale price ($2) gives a total revenue of $20, but the higher quantity 15, multiplied by the new lower price of only $1, leads to revenue of only $15.

There is a neat geometric device by which changes in total revenue can be seen at a glance from Figure 6–5. Remember that TR = P × Q. Here OP is a vertical side of a rectangle while OQ is a horizontal side of the same rectangle. Euclid proved that multiplying two sides of a rectangle gives the area of the

FIGURE 6–5

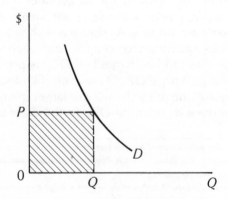

FIGURE 6–6

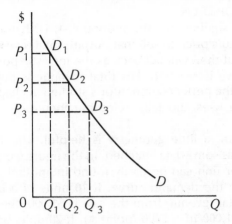

rectangle (shaded in the diagram). Hence the shaded area represents total revenue.

Note what the monopoly finds as it raises its output from zero (Figure 6–6). The rising quantity and falling price bring higher total revenue for a time—we can see that rectangle $OP_1D_1Q_1$ is smaller than $OP_2D_2Q_2$, which is in turn smaller than $OP_3D_3Q_3$. Economists call the region where lower price brings higher total revenue (and vice versa) the *elastic* portion of the demand curve. There is another region, however, where reducing price brings *lower* total revenue (and vice versa); this is the *inelastic* portion of the demand curve. Figure 6–7 illustrates

FIGURE 6–7

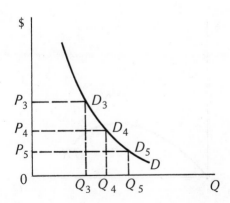

how rectangle OP₃D₃Q₃ is larger than OP₄D₄Q₄ and much larger than OP₅D₅Q₅.

What this signifies for the monopolist, is that as he raises output and cuts price to sell that output, total revenue will rise for a time but then will fall back as the inelastic portion of the demand curve is reached. His total revenue is not a straight line, as was the perfect competitor's studied in chapter 4, but a curve which rises and falls as output increases. (See Figure 6–8.)

Once again, a little geometry is helpful. The TR curve in Figure 6–9 has some data attached. In the figure we can see that the price per unit can be easily found in another manner, as well as from the demand curve. If 10 units of a product are sold, and total revenue from the sale is $1,000, then the price per unit is $1,000/10 = $100 (point A). If 20 units bring $1,800, unit price has dropped to $1,800/20 = $90 (point B). Similarly, price is $2,400/40 = $60 at point C, $3,000/60 = $50 at point D, $3,200/80 = $40 at point E, and $3,000/100 = $30 at point F. In every case the slope of a straight line from the origin to the point shows the price. OE, for example, has a numerical slope of $3,200/80 = $40, while OF, which is obviously less steep, has a slope of $3,000/100 = $30. Thus price per unit can be found (1) directly on the demand curve, or (2) by the slope of a straight line from the origin to the TR curve.

The monopolist's cost curve, on the other hand, presents no difficulties. Its slope is identical to the perfect competitor's already seen and duplicated here in Figure 6–10.

FIGURE 6–8

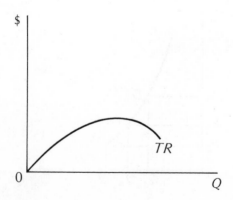

FIGURE 6–9

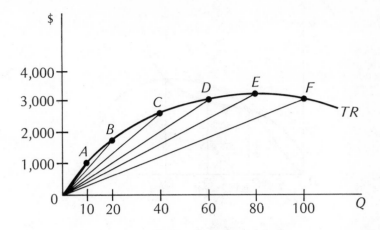

To find the quantity and price that will maximize profits for the monopolist, we must superimpose the TR curve and the TC curve as in Figure 6–11. As with the competitor, the level of output which brings maximum profits is found at the point where the vertical distance between TC and TR is the greatest (since TR − TC = total profits). The diagram shows that abnormal profits are earned when the firm produces more than OQ_{be1} but less than OQ_{be2}, the break-even points. Abnormal profits are maximized when the firm produces OQ_m, the point where the longest vertical line can be drawn between TR and

FIGURE 6–10

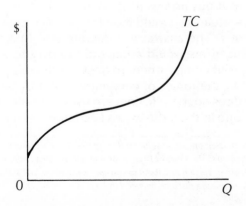

FIGURE 6–11

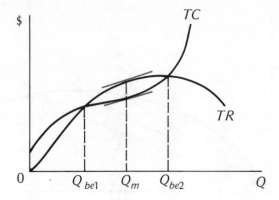

TC.[6] To sell the quantity OQm, the monopoly must charge a price OPm as seen from its demand curve in Figure 6–12.

WHAT ARE THE ECONOMIC PROBLEMS OF MONOPOLY

We now know how to make the price and quantity decisions that maximize profit for the monopolist. Thus far, both the diagrams and the logic used to explain them have been innocent enough. But monopoly is inherently unfavorable to the consuming public in several major respects.

Consider Figure 6–11 once again. We saw that the monopoly would produce the quantity OQm which would maximize profits for it. If this firm were suddenly shifted into a perfectly competitive situation, would it be forced to change its production decisions? The answer is a definite yes. In a competitive environment, firms would enter the industry to share in the abnormal profit being earned. In the long run this profit will be eliminated by the forces of competition. But by definition the monopoly does not have to concern itself with other firms, as it is the only one in the industry. As such, there is no reason why

---

[6] *Once again, tangent lines are useful for finding this point accurately. Only at OQm is the slope of TC equal to the slope of TR, as shown in red. The lines have ended their trend away from each other, and are just about to converge once more. But at that point they are parallel, and therefore the distance between them is at a maximum.*

FIGURE 6–12

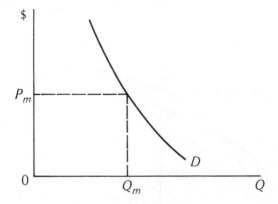

its abnormal profitability should not continue even in the long run.

The possible permanence of monopoly profits means automatically that the distribution of income in society is different from what it would be in a competitive framework. Monopoly profits come from the pockets of the consumer, and end up in the pockets of the owners (stockholders) of the monopoly.

The nonexistence of competition is unfavorable in another regard. Monopolies by their very nature have little motivation to modernize or to eliminate existing inefficiencies. Since profits are above normal anyway, the monopolist would rather let his old equipment wear out before replacing it even if more efficient designs become available. With the spur of competition absent, stagnation, obsolete plant and equipment, and "don't rock the boat" entrepreneurship can be typical behavior, as seen especially with many public utilities and a good number of US railroads which are regulated monopolies in their area.

Finally, it is likely that a monopoly will choose to produce less and charge a higher price than will the firms in a competitive industry. In Figure 6–13, profits are maximized at quantity OQ_m. But what if the industry were perfectly competitive, so that taken together all the hundreds of participating firms had the same total cost curve TC as in the diagram? The situation would then be different. Competitive pressures would eliminate abnormal profit and cause production to occur at the

FIGURE 6–13

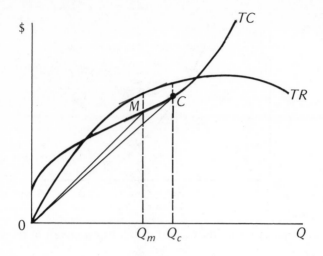

quantity that minimizes cost per unit. In the figure, this is at quantity OQc, with unit cost represented by the tangent line OC.[7] Thus, given the same cost curve, a monopoly will choose to restrict output below the competitive level because that maximizes profits for it.

The production of a smaller quantity than that which minimizes unit costs automatically means higher cost output for the monopoly than for the competitive firm. See how the slope of OM is steeper than that of OC, representing greater cost per unit of output at the monopolist's chosen production point.

Since output is reduced by the monopoly, a higher price can be charged for its product. Figure 6–14 shows the market price OPc in a perfectly competitive industry. If the industry is monopolized by one firm which produces less (OQm), then the price it charges consumers will be higher too (OPm).[8]

---

[7] Recall that the slope of a line from the origin to TC shows cost per unit. OC is the shallowest line that can be drawn to TC, it being just tangent. Hence unit costs are minimized at OQc.

[8] Under special conditions of exceptionally great scale economies, the predictions of lower output, higher cost, and higher price might not hold true. Some people think that a monopoly will charge the highest price it can get, which is not true. At such a price there would be few buyers and profits would disappear. The price which maximizes profits will be far lower than the highest possible price.

FIGURE 6–14

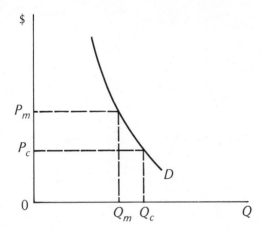

The permanence of abnormal profits, resulting inequalities of income distribution, stagnant behavior involving long-run cost inefficiencies, lower output, higher costs, and higher prices—all in all a serious indictment of monopoly.

PRICE DISCRIMINATION

The assumption thus far has been that the monopolist charges only one price for his product. Under certain circumstances, it may be even more profitable for different rates to be charged to separate buyers. This is called "price discrimination." Say two groups, adults and children, have very different demand for a product such as movie tickets. Those responsible for ticket prices will first find it advantageous to estimate what the respective demand curves look like. For children, the curve will undoubtedly be elastic, with moderate price reductions leading to large increases in movie attendance and vice-versa. For adults, who are more wealthy as a group, the demand will be inelastic, as adults will not be so concerned with ticket prices, and rises or falls in the price will not alter attendance as much. Two curves reflecting this are shown in Figure 6–15. It is thus seen that various prices and quantities will give very different total revenues for each class of consumer. Profit can be maximized independently within each group by charging different prices—higher for adults and lower for children.

FIGURE 6–15

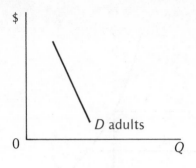

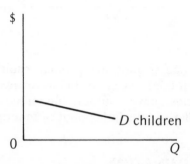

Only a few sellers discriminate: some examples are airlines with youth fares, electric companies which charge different rates depending on consumption, and doctors who charge rich patients more than poor. What do they all have in common?

First, they all have the ability to segregate a market into independent groups: age for the cinema and the airline with its youth fares; amount purchased for the electric company charging different rates depending on consumption; income of patients for the doctor who charges rich patients more than poor; time for the motel with off-season rates or the restaurant with lower lunch prices; and geographical location for the drug firm which charged your author 30¢ in Istanbul for the same nose drops that cost him $2.90 in the US.

Second, the ability to compartmentalize a market must be there. If resale is possible, then price discrimination cannot work. The child who buys the cheap movie ticket, if he could sell it to the adult at a price a little above what he paid for it, could turn a profit. He would have a nice business going except that the adult, too recognizable by the movie management, could not get away with it. The rule, then, is that where resale is difficult or impossible (the doctor's services, delivered electric power, etc.) then price discrimination can flourish. Otherwise it will not.

In short, the economic problems which monopoly inflicts on society are worsened when the monopoly can engage in price discrimination.

Questions

1. How do firms acquire control over price?
2. How does a monopoly's decisions as to what price to charge and what quantity to produce differ from a perfectly competitive firm's? Why?
3. What economic problems does a monopoly cause for society?
4. Why do some firms engage in price discrimination? When can they do so?

7.

MARKET POWER
IN THE 1970s:
Monopolistic Competition
and Oligopoly

Perfect competition is relatively rare in the American economy of the 1970s, but so is unregulated monopoly. Business organization today is usually a combination of the two. Some industries may be highly but not perfectly competitive, with a limited degree of market power. In the 1930s, Professor E. H. Chamberlin of Harvard coined the term "monopolistic competition" to describe this situation. On the other hand, some large firms which are not monopolies may face only a handful of competing firms, and may possess substantial market power. Such an industry is an "oligopoly," derived from the Greek *oligos polein*, meaning a few sellers. This chapter will explore these two conditions.

MONOPOLISTIC COMPETITION

Many American industries are monopolistically competitive, with a fairly large number of firms having relatively easy entry to and exit from the industry. The great number of firms makes price agreements and other collusion between them virtually impossible. A major characteristic of monopolistic competition is the attempt of firms to *differentiate their product*. The consuming public might be convinced that there is some difference, real or imagined, in the good being sold. If so, then like the monopoly case but unlike perfect competition, a rise in price will reduce demand but not eliminate it entirely. There are many ways to foster differences in the product, such as introducing changes in quality, whether great or slight, or using advertising, brand names, and attractive packaging. The location of the store or factory, its credit policy, the courtesy of the clerks and salespeople, service and warranty arrangements, all mean that demand will not be perfectly elastic, but will have some slope as in Figure 7–1.

FIGURE 7–1

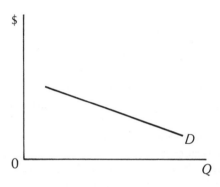

Monopolistic competition is very common in retailing, where groceries, hardware, cleaning supplies, haircuts, clothing, gas, lumber, and home appliances fit our description well.[1] The limited degree of market power in these cases means that prices will be relatively uniform between competing products.

In the short run, aside from the fact that demand is likely to be more elastic, the monopolistically competitive firm's price and quantity decisions will be like a monopoly's. It will maximize profit by producing at the point where $TR - TC$ is greatest (OQ_m in Figure 7–2). The situation pictured will not be a permanent one, however.

Figure 7–2 shows attractive abnormal profit being earned, while one of the characteristics of monopolistic competition was easy entry into the industry. Entrepreneurs earning only

---

[1] An industry may be monopolistically competitive in some situations yet be more powerful elsewhere. Jackman, Maine had one doctor at last count—the only one within 60 miles—while Los Angeles has thousands. There are only a few taxi companies in New York City, and dozens in Washington D.C.

FIGURE 7–2

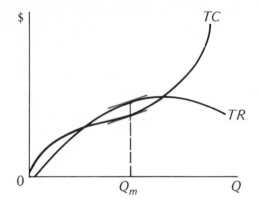

normal profits elsewhere will be tempted to share in the high returns by entering the field. The new competition will have serious results for firms already established. A firm where the demand for a product was D_1 in Figure 7–3 is now likely to find that demand reduced, say to D_2, no matter what price it charges. In turn, this means less total revenue for any quantity produced. Notice that if the firm produced OQ_1, its total revenue would decline from rectangle $OWXQ_1$ to rectangle $OYZQ_1$. (The shaded portion of the diagram shows the lost total revenue for the firm.)

If many new firms enter the industry, the resulting decline in total revenue for any individual firm may be quite large, as shown in Figure 7–4. In this case, there is no conceivable com-

FIGURE 7–3

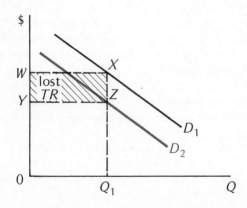

FIGURE 7–4

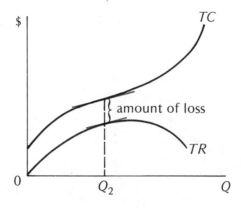

bination of output and price that would give a profit. TR is always below TC, and the best the firm can do is to minimize its losses by producing OQ_2.

Now the incentives are reversed. Firms are incurring losses. Some firms—the weakest, perhaps, or those whose managers most quickly perceive profit opportunities elsewhere—will leave the industry. Surviving firms will therefore find the demand for their individual product rising, and total revenue will be higher no matter what the quantity sold.

There is only one circumstance in which new firms will not enter the industry seeking high profit, nor old firms leave it to avoid losses. This is when existing firms are earning only normal profit, just sufficient to keep them in the business. As Figure 7–5 shows, this situation occurs when the TR curve is just tangent to the TC curve, so that neither abnormal profit nor losses are present.[2] This is long-run equilibrium under monopolistic competition.

The firm produces a quantity OQ_{mc}, and sells each unit at a price of OA, which is exactly the same as cost per unit (including normal profit).

The untutored observer will now say, "Ah, monopolistic competition is thus a good thing. Monopoly profits are eliminated, and the selling price is just equal to unit cost—exactly the same as under perfect competition." It seems in textbooks

---

[2] *Economists call this the "tangency solution" for long-run equilibrium under monopolistic competition.*

FIGURE 7–5

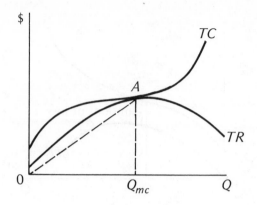

that untutored observers are always wrong, and that is the case here. Look closely once again at the diagram, and at its twin in Figure 7–6. If this firm had been *perfectly* competitive, then in the long run it would have produced the quantity that minimizes cost per unit. In Figure 7–6, this point is at quantity OQ_c, with unit costs represented by the tangent line OC.

But the monopolistically competitive firm will produce *less* than OQ_c, at OQ_{mc}. The production of a smaller quantity than that which minimizes unit costs automatically means higher cost output under monopolistic competition. See how the slope of OM is steeper than that of OC, and thus represents greater cost per unit of output at the monopolistic competitor's chosen production point.

FIGURE 7–6

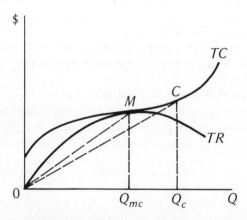

Since output is reduced below the competitive level, a higher price will be charged for the product. Figure 7-7 shows the market price OP$_c$ in a perfectly competitive industry. If the industry is monopolistically competitive, producing less as at OQ$_{mc}$, then the price paid by consumers will be higher too (OP$_{mc}$). True, abnormal profit is eliminated. But in the long run, price is higher and output is less than under perfect competition. Finally, there are two circumstances in which monopolistic competition may be even less favorable than monopoly for society. Consider the needless waste caused by movements into a profitable industry. We saw that profit is quickly converted into loss when too many firms flock to share the presumed reward. The city intersection with one thriving gas station ends up with four—one on each corner. A common result is that one or two of the stations fail to make a go of it, and the empty shell of their buildings marked "closed" is mute testimony to the possible wastes of monopolistic competition. Also, we have seen that firms will attempt to differentiate their product. To the extent that spurious or unimportant quality change, advertising, and other marketing tactics are used, their costs will have to be borne by the consuming public. (Both advertising and quality change are discussed more fully in chapter 8.) It is often argued that these costs are offset by the consumer's ability to choose among a large selection of slightly different products. Brand names will engender trust and confidence, it is said. Readers must decide for themselves whether these benefits outweigh the costs of monopolistic competition.

FIGURE 7-7

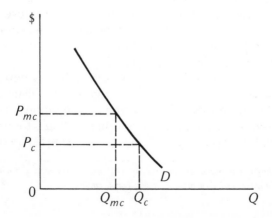

One further point should be made. The long-run equilibrium where abnormal profits are competed away is inherently unstable. At any time firms can seek increased profits by additional advertising, by instituting quality change, and so forth. If they succeed, the whole process of competing away profit by means of the entry of new firms will begin anew. Rather than saying that there is a long-run equilibrium in monopolistic competition, it is more accurate to think of a tendency toward an equilibrium being continuously upset by profit-seeking entrepreneurs.

OLIGOPOLIES IN THE 1970s

When people speak of big business, giant corporations, or multinational enterprise, they are usually speaking of firms in an oligopolistic industry. Oligopoly as we have seen means a few sellers, and that is the chief characteristic of this form of organization. One of the easiest ways to detect whether an industry is an oligopoly, with a potential for market control, is to determine that industry's "concentration ratio." This commonly-used tool shows the fraction of an industry's total output that is controlled by the largest four (or occasionally eight) sellers. Some sample four-firm concentration ratios are aluminum 100, automobiles 99, electric light bulbs 92, synthetic fibres 82, cigarettes 80, soap and detergents 72, and tires and tubes 70.[3] There is no doubt that these industries are oligopolies.

The high degree of concentration and the large size of firms in an oligopolistic industry indicate serious obstacles to the entry of potential competitors, as discussed earlier. In particular, when firms have grown to the size of those whose concentration ratios were just noted, there must be great economies of scale in production. If so, interlopers face high capital costs if they want to consider competing.

Unfortunately, the theory of oligopoly is less certain in its prediction than was true of perfect and monopolistic competition, and of monopoly. Several types of oligopoly exist which are different enough from one another so that a theory covering them all has to be quite general. For example, an oligopoly

---

[3] See Senate Subcommittee on Antitrust and Monopoly, Concentration Ratios in Manufacturing Industry, 1963 (Washington, 1966), part I, table 2.

may consist of as few as two firms, or there may be two dozen. Intuition tells us that an industry of only two firms will behave quite differently from one with many firms. A further difficulty is that some oligopolistic firms try hard to differentiate their product (for example, cars or cigarettes) while other firms produce a completely standard product like cement or steel.[4] Finally, there may be collusion between firms—the unsavory world of "cartels," "pools," "trusts," and "gentlemen's agreements"—or again there may be no collusion. These differences mean that the theory of oligopoly is neither neat nor sharply defined, and more advanced texts explore these special cases in more detail.

Oligopolies do have one noticeable characteristic, however. In the absence of agreements between firms, an entrepreneur never knows exactly how his rivals will react to a price or output change that he himself makes. In fact, one good definition of oligopoly is an industry where the number of firms is sufficiently small so that any market decision made by one firm must take into account the reaction of its adversaries. Economists call this situation "mutual dependence" or "interdependence." An example would be a firm that unilaterally raises its selling price. If the three, five, or ten other firms in the oligopoly do not follow along, then the firm which raised prices is likely to lose a large quantity of sales. A manager needs all the information he can get as to whether rivals will raise prices or not if he makes the first move. What if our same manager wants to stimulate sales by lowering his price? This seems simple enough—consumers will purchase more goods at the reduced price. But this does not consider the reaction of the other firms; rather than lose trade, they may prefer to lower their price, too. If so, the first firm will discover that its sales increases are small.

A diagrammatic picture of this situation is shown in Figure 7–8. This is a "kinked" demand curve for a single oligopolistic firm. The shape of the curve implies that the firm will hesitate to rock the boat by changing price. Any decision to raise prices above OP_0 will rapidly reduce sales and total revenue. The portion of the demand curve above the kink is highly elastic; as already noted, competing firms might not go along with the price increase. Conversely, a price decrease by the firm shown in the diagram may be followed by competing firms which do

---

[4] *The names imperfect and perfect oligopoly are sometimes applied to these two cases.*

FIGURE 7–8

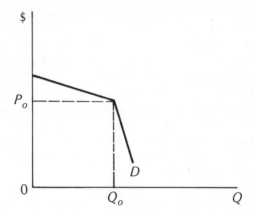

not wish to lose trade. The reduction in price may thus not increase quantity by very much, and along this inelastic portion of the demand curve total revenue will fall off quickly.

The main implication of the kink is that an oligopolistic firm will be reluctant to initiate a price or quantity change. Revenues may drop off sharply, whether prices and quantities are raised or lowered. TR itself exhibits a kink, as in Figure 7–9. Any decision to produce more or less than OQ_0 sharply reduces revenue on either side of A. As TR peaks so abruptly, notice that even large cost changes (increases from TC_1 to TC_2, decreases from TC_1 to TC_3) will still leave profits maximized at quantity OQ_0. The kink both in demand and in total revenue

FIGURE 7–9

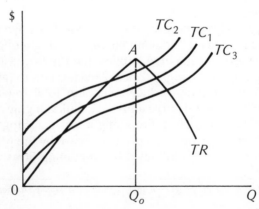

thus helps to explain why any single oligopolistic firm has a vested interest in market stability.

Kinked curves are useful for showing stability, although there is one weakness: we do not know why the kink occurs precisely where it does. Why not at some higher price and lower output, or the reverse? The answer involves the history of an industry's development—its debates, negotiations, price wars, peace treaties, personal friendships and animosities—in short, any relevant factors which bind together rival firms in an industrial price pattern.

Yet, oligopolies do change their prices (as anyone who buys gasoline in the 1970s can attest). One possibility is where all firms in the industry are subjected to a cost change at the same time. A new industry-wide labor contract might apply uniformly, raising wage bills simultaneously for all firms. Tax rate increases might be voted by Congress, or the Federal Reserve Board might engineer higher interest rates across the economy. Shortages of raw materials (crude oil, for example) might occur for all firms at the same time. Under these conditions, managers are likely to make price increases at the same time in the reasonable expectation that all other firms will follow.

It is obvious that one firm's predictions of what another firm will do is a key part of its decision-making process. In recent years, the mathematical theory of games has been applied to this problem. Game theory uses the mathematics of probability in conflict situations, and puts prediction on a more scientific basis.[5] Practitioners of the theory seem to have a bright future on the staffs of the large corporations.

There is one illegal or quasi-legal way in which these puzzles may be solved, especially when the number of firms is quite small. That is when firms enter into collusion with one another by means of formal or informal agreements (kept secret, of course, when they are against the law, as is usually the case in the US). The lessons learned in our study of monopoly are helpful in this case. If three of four firms can agree to act as one, adding together their total cost and revenue, they can then find the monopoly price and quantity that maximizes

---

[5] *Formulated by John von Neumann and Oskar Morgenstern, the first article on game theory (1928) described a rational strategy for matching pennies. From these humble beginnings, the theory has become useful in analyzing war and politics as well as conflict among firms in an oligopolistic industry. (Von Neumann's daughter, incidentally, became the first female member of the President's Council of Economic Advisors in 1972.)*

profits for the group as a whole. Problems may occur when some firms have relatively high costs while others are more economical in operation. What then? A compromise might be reached in which both sides deviate from their individual profit maximization points to gain the benefits of industrial peace. Most of the benefits of collusion can actually be obtained even without agreements among firms. It is quite common to find a system of *price leadership* in oligopolistic industries. The largest (or sometimes the most influential or prestigious) firm in an industry may make its market decisions independently of other firms. The remaining firms in the industry will then as a matter of course duplicate the largest firm's decisions. The latter will presumably maximize its own individual profits. If these others face similar costs and demand curves, they will obtain the same thing. On the other hand, firms with higher costs will have to sacrifice some profits, although they may find this far preferable to the uncertainties of competition. Price leadership is usually held to be legal by the courts, hence its common occurrence in industries like steel, gasoline, cigarettes, and many more.

What are the basic pros and cons of oligopoly? Supporters emphasize the success of oligopolies at achieving economies of scale. A perfectly competitive firm cannot attain the quantity of output needed to bring unit costs down, so prices cannot be as low for the consumer. Further, profits earned by oligopolies can be used to finance expensive research, which could not be afforded by more competitive firms. There is an incentive to use innovations at once, because the product can be further differentiated by quality change without provoking a price war. Introducing a new model or a new line embodying quality change, but at a higher price, is far safer than competitive price increases on goods already produced. The reaction of rivals is to institute their own quality change, all to the consumer's benefit. In any case, research and technical progress is a good bet. If they should turn out to be profitable, the rewards could last a long time because of the difficulties facing new firms which want to enter the industry.

Opponents of oligopoly attempt to refute both these main arguments, and believe that oligopolies can be even worse for society than if all industries were monopolized. The "economies of scale" argument noted above sounds persuasive. However, it is not valid to claim that lower costs necessarily mean lower prices for consumers. The element of abnormal profit should not be forgotten. Whether lower costs mean lower prices depends on profit rates in the industry. Each industry will have to be looked at separately to see if economies of scale have actually benefited the consumer. In addition, opponents say that like monopoly, oligopoly restricts output below that which would give *minimum* unit costs. This in turn means higher prices than would be possible at the greater output level.

"Oligopolies as the fountainhead of American research" is a tangled question on which many authorities have debated for years. On the evidence, the research establishments of large corporations have *not* overshadowed the efforts of small research institutions and independent inventors. An indication of this is a recent report of the government advisory group on technological innovation headed by Robert A. Charpie, then of Union Carbide. The Charpie Report cited several studies showing that independent inventors and small companies "are responsible for a remarkable percent of the important inventions and innovations of this century—a much larger percent than their relative investment in these activities suggest."

Many major inventions sound certain to have emanated from large research establishments, among them air conditioning, power steering, Xerography, the cyclotron, cotton picker, helicopter, FM radio circuitry, automatic transmissions, the zipper, shrink-proof knitwear, the kodachrome process, the polaroid camera, cellophane, continuous hot strip rolling of steel, oxygen steelmaking, and seven major inventions in refining and cracking petroleum. Yet all of those inventions came from lone inventors or small firms. Even when the output of the large research establishments is relatively disappointing, this can be camouflaged with good public relations, press agentry, and marketing. One investigator, Donald Schon, argues that:

> DuPont . . . owes its success more to its phenomenal ability to carry out market and engineering development of inventions derived from other sources than its own research output. IBM, the present giant of the computer field, was not the first to enter into the development of electronic computers; it waited, sticking with its older punch card systems, until other firms had built and marketed computers, and only then moved in, with great marketing and technical service resources and skills, to dominate the field.[6]

---

[6] *See* Donald A. Schon, Technology and Change *(New York: Delacorte, 1967), pp. 117–18.*

Apropos of this last point, the head of IBM has stated:

> The disc memory unit, the heart of today's random access computer, is not the logical outcome of a decision made by IBM management. It was developed in one of our laboratories as a bootlegged project—over the stern warning from management that the project had to be dropped because of budget difficulties. A handful of men ignored the warning. They broke the rules. They risked their jobs to work on a project they believed in.[7]

Even where the oligopolistic laboratories *are* fruitful, there is another complication. In some industries—aerospace, telecommunications, and electrical equipment, for example—considerably more than half the spending on research has been financed by the federal government. With government making the payments, it is surely stretching things to give full credit for research accomplishments in these areas to the oligopolists. In short, although oligopolies have swiftly adopted many major inventions and marketed them with ability, their claim to be the fountainhead of research is at best highly debatable.

The accusation made by opponents of oligopoly that in some ways oligopolies are actually worse than monopoly for society falls into five categories:

1. Oligopoly may be less efficient than monopoly. A monopoly can build plants that exploit economies of scale as far as possible. But where there are several separate firms, each may be too small in size to obtain maximum scale economies.

2. If reductions in cost occur for a single oligopolistic firm, it may hesitate to lower its price (remember the kinked demand curve, and the fear of price wars). But this is not an obstacle for a monopoly, which will happily lower its price when this adds to profits.

3. When they exist, monopolies are very often regulated as public utilities.

4. In some cases, there will be less variety in the product. Radio broadcasting in a small city is a good example. Assume surveys show that at 4 PM, four-fifths of the potential audience want to hear country and western music, while one-fifth want

---

[7] *Ibid., p. 170.*

to hear classical music. If there were two stations in the community, both would obviously broadcast country and western. If instead there were a monopoly station broadcasting two programs, then it could maximize its audience (and profits) by scheduling one country and western and one classical program at the same time.

5. The final objection is perhaps the most compelling. In oligopoly, advertising that does not inform and quality change that is not real is at its most common. These topics receive specific treatment in the next chapter.

Questions

1. What is monopolistic competition? Would you prefer to live in an economy organized in this way? Why or why not?
2. What is oligopoly? Make a case for it and against it.
3. What is the importance of the "kinked curve" in the theory of oligopoly?
4. Why is it sometimes said that oligopolies may be worse for society than monopolies?

8.

ADVERTISING AND QUALITY CHANGE

Product differentiation is pursued in both monopolistic competition and oligopoly. Firms in industries of both types advertise avidly and introduce quality change, real or illusory, on a more or less permanent basis. But only the large oligopolistic corporations have the resources to conduct campaigns of this kind on a national or international scale, hence most interest centers on such firms. However the following can apply as much to monopolistic competition as to oligopoly.

ADVERTISING

Advertising is often a very effective non-price method for improving a firm's position. As an enormous $21 billion business (about half of what we spend on US public education through high school), it is the target of much criticism. The first historical evidence of advertising comes from Egyptian Thebes 3000 years ago, where public criers handled the job. The word advertising is of much more recent vintage. In Shakespeare's day it meant "general news," while its present usage can be dated from September 14, 1710, when the *Tatler* suggested using it for business purposes only. Problems with this industry are hardly new. In 1758 Dr. Samuel Johnson wrote, "Advertisements are now so numerous that they are very negligently perused, and it is therefore become necessary to gain attention by magnificence of promise and by eloquence sometimes sublime and sometimes pathetick."

Textbooks on advertising single out various categories of appeal to customers, such as sex, food and drink, personal comforts, freedom from fear and danger, desire to be superior ("trade up to a Pontiac"), social approval, long life and love of family.

Among economists, advertising can be a controversial subject that generates many differences of opinion. Some of these include:

1. Does advertising give useful information about a product, educating the buying public and bringing more competition to a market? Or by artificially stimulating wants, does it persuade the public to buy goods it really doesn't want? There is truth on both sides. Informative advertising which calls attention to price differences, new firms, and new products is certainly valuable in a world of imperfect competition. Many ads in daily newspapers fit this description. But at their worst, ads give no information of value, attempt to catch attention by subtle or blatant annoyance (for example, louder volume on TV, endless repetition) and descend like the old carnival pitch-man's spiel to half-truths or less. Whenever this results in consumers purchasing advertised goods of lower quality or higher price in place of unadvertised but cheaper and better goods, then there is cause for social concern. Non-informative techniques have recently come in for much criticism. "Spontaneous" man-on-the-street testimony which is staged, and the "puff" are two main offenders. The puff is a meaningless statement which nevertheless sounds appealing. For example, one detergent washes clothes "whiter than white," another goes "all the way beyond white." Gasoline can come in a "big big gallon," tires last "30,000 long miles," soap powder makes "30 percent more active suds" and one brand of panty hose lasts "50 percent longer" (than what?).

The Federal Trade Commission's case file contains some true ad classics. Contac Nasal Spray was applied to rice paper along with a competing product; the Contac soaked in. The F.T.C. complained about the relation between that and easier penetration of the mucous membrane. No, said the producer, we were not trying to show that, only that Contac had a bottle with a bigger hole! Using a safety razor, a man was shown shaving sandpaper after Rapid-Shave had been applied. The F.T.C. showed that the sand was on glass! In another ad, Libby-Owens-Ford glass in autos was seen to possess remarkable clarity. No wonder: the F.T.C. found that the car windows were rolled down. Libby-Owens-Ford stated that this was because it was raining on the day the ad was filmed!

Certain forms of advertising carry additional costs for society.[1] Billboards which pollute scenery are a good example. Motorists crossing the Pyrenees Mountains receive quite a shock when, still on French soil where billboards are strictly controlled, they catch a first glimpse of Spain with its lower standards of regulation: billboards crown the ridges up from the road like a modern-day Great Wall. US efforts at control of signs started with Hawaii, then still a territory, before World War II. Vermont's present law is strict and well-known, although in most states the billboard lobby is strong and "scenic pollution" remains very common. Offense may also be given by ads for mouthwash, underarm wetness, girdles and bras with women squirming therein, and dentures where the audience is treated to a successful bite and noisy mastication. That all viewers do not find TV ads gripping fare is shown by the well-documented sudden large rise in New York City water consumption at the same time commercials are broadcast in prime-time.[2]

2. Does advertising lead to higher output and thus economies of scale, or does it raise costs and price? Depending on the situation, the answer could be yes in both cases. Figure 8–1 shows a quantity OQ_w being produced without advertising. With advertising, a firm may be able to sell more output, say OQ_a. Of course the costs of the advertising must now be met. If an ad campaign costs \$100,000, then we must move TC_1 vertically upward by that amount all along its length (to TC_2). Nevertheless, the larger output allows for economies of scale, and cost per unit of output falls in this case from the slope of OW to the lower slope of OA, and lower unit costs will allow consumers to obtain the product at a lower price.

But this is an optimistic scenario. It implies a successful ad campaign that has allowed a single firm to obtain and to keep a big increase in its market. The situation would look different if rivals retaliate with their own successful advertising. If all firms mount equally effective ad campaigns, the result would be an increase in a firm's costs without an increase in output as shown in Figure 8–2. The effect is then to raise prices, not to lower them. It seems reasonable to suppose that this latter

---

[1] *The concept of social cost is analyzed more fully in chapter 10.*

[2] *In Europe, TV ads are often limited to a once-per-hour time period, with no interruption of scheduled programming.*

FIGURE 8–1

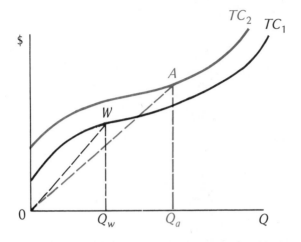

case—one firm's ad success being offset by its competitors —will be fairly common.[3] Why advertise under these conditions? The answer is a key to understanding the use of advertising: a *temporary* increase in demand will be experienced by the firm that gets favorable results from its ads. True, this will not be permanent; but before other firms react and reply, there are profits to be made.

Figure 8–3 shows how total revenue rises after advertising from TR_1 to TR_2. (A demand increase for the product leads to higher TR at any given price and quantity.) Meanwhile, total costs have risen from TC_1 to TC_2 because of the advertising. Profits have risen from a relatively low level at their maximum without advertising (AB at OQ_1 output) to the high level YZ at output OQ_2, which is the maximum attainable profit after advertising. Even if these gains are eventually lost as competitors respond, the larger profit YZ has been flowing into the firm's pockets for a period of time. That is why a rational businessman will advertise even if he knows the advantages may be transitory.

3. Does advertising promote more spending, leading to full employment, or does it overemphasize the private economy at

---

[3] *An exception will occur when all firms advertising together increase their sales because consumers switch their purchases away from other products. In this case scale economies will be possible after all. However, diseconomies of scale in the industries forced to reduce their output must then be considered also.*

FIGURE 8–2

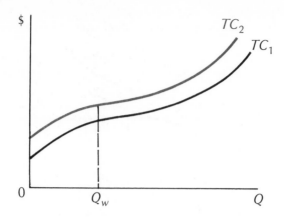

the expense of the public welfare? Proponents argue that without ads creating wants, the market for goods would be depressed and employment would suffer. Opponents respond that there is little evidence to support this view. Advertising does indeed powerfully affect the *mix* of what is consumed, causing large changes in the demand for particular goods. But there is much less impact on the totality of spending as compared to saving. There is surprising stability in the percent of income spent and saved, both over long time periods when the

FIGURE 8–3

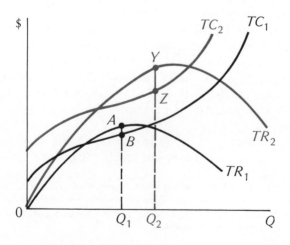

advertising industry has grown relative to the economy, and between countries where that industry varies in size.[4]

Opponents further contend that the main shift in consumption which does occur because of advertising is away from the public sector of the economy to the private sector. John Kenneth Galbraith, well-known Harvard economist, first publicized this argument in the late 1950s and impressive evidence exists to support it. The project or cause that is not profitable for private enterprise will not be advertised. Thus, with the exception of some public service ads, the occasional government-sponsored health or safety ad, and the work of pressure groups like Common Cause or the Sierra Club—all strictly limited by budget constraints—output of goods and new ideas in the public sector do not get advertised. Covered under this rubric are public schools, preservation of wilderness, medical research, control of population, urban transport systems, and the like. If advertising is effective, says Galbraith, then there will be overemphasis on private goods and too little spending on public goods.

This argument can be taken one further step. Because it is not profitable to do so, there is little or no advertising for *less* consumption. The 1970s have seen crises in electric power, gasoline consumption, the proliferation of wastes such as bottles and cans, and others. Who has both the will and the resources to advertise *curtailing* the output and use of these products? Some people feel that government must play a greater role in this regard, but obviously this is a ticklish area of political concern.

4. Supporters say that advertising gives us free radio and TV programs.[5] Opponents say, oh no, we pay all right. The truth lies in between. Ad revenues do allow us to receive such signals without putting a coin in the slot and without paying a tax on the receiver (as is often the case in foreign countries such as Great Britain, where the tax on TVs is now £7 for black and white and £12 for color TV per year, used to support the British Broadcasting Corporation). On the other hand, where costs and prices are raised by advertising, then the consumer of the

---

[4] *Reasons for this stability are discussed in chapter 4 of the author's Managing the Modern Economy. One reason may be that banks and other savings institutions advertise too.*

[5] *Also much cheaper magazines and newspapers.*

product pays for the radio and TV programs. This leads to the unusual situation where some who pay don't watch, some who don't pay do watch, and some both pay and watch.

How much should a firm spend on advertising? Is there any general rule to guide the businessman? The answer is to aim as usual for profit maximization. The costs of the campaign can be estimated accurately. The effect on the firm's total revenue will be much harder to predict, but some estimate can be made. The firm should spend on advertising up to the point where the costs of the ads plus costs of production, subtracted from sales revenue, is at a maximum.

QUALITY CHANGE

Quality change can be analyzed in much the same way as advertising. As with advertising, it is more important as a means of competition than price changes in some industries. Quality change sounds desirable, like apple pie (and motherhood until recently). And desirable it may be in cases where appealing variety is introduced into a product: where safer, less noisy, energy-conserving, more durable, more effective goods are made available.

The disadvantage of quality change comes when, in combination with advertising, marginal or ephemeral changes are emphasized and the consumer is convinced that a real improvement has been embodied. Yearly model changes in certain industries have attracted particularly adverse comment. Many annual "improvements" in automobiles, appliances, snowmobiles, motorboats, clothing, and the like seem like gimmickry to the critics. Soaps, detergents, deodorants, shaving supplies, and cigarettes also receive their share of criticism for perpetrating "quality hokum" on the consumer.

Trading stamps and games such as Bonus Bingo, Match the Presidents, Sunny Dollars, and Supermarket Sweepstakes can all be considered as a form of quality change. A sack of flour in the store must be treated differently depending upon whether it comes with or without trading stamps, a Bonus Bingo ticket, and so on. Games have been under legislative attack in recent years. According to Congressional testimony in 1970, the cost of games pushes up prices to consumers by an average of 7 percent. Abuses in the management of such games include hidden clauses or rules which make winning difficult, payouts which are far below the announced figure (38 percent for a petroleum corporation, 3 percent for a hamburger chain), and winning tickets which are not randomly mixed.[6] As a result, in 1968 Maryland banned gas station games, and since then state government controls and prohibitions have proliferated.

How much should an entrepreneur spend on quality change? The logic is the same as for advertising. Estimate costs and expected revenue from the change, include them with the firm's total cost and total revenue calculations, and select that level of quality change which maximizes the difference (profits).

Questions

1. Does advertising lead to economies of scale, or does it cause higher costs and higher prices?
2. Higher profits from advertising and quality change may well not be permanent. As they raise costs, why then engage in them?
3. How much should a firm spend on advertising and quality change?

APPENDIX
Is it Justifiable to Say Firms Maximize Profits?

Our theory of how a firm behaves has been based throughout on the assumption that it wants to maximize its profits. This assumption has had crucial implications for our overall view of

---

[6] *In the community where the author shops, a local supermarket announced a sweepstakes game with winning tickets bringing prizes ranging from $1 to $1000. The author and some friends predicted that a $1000 winning ticket would turn up on the first day of the game, and that there would not be another one. We were wrong: the only $1000 winner came up on the fourth day.*

the market system. The search for profit spurs competition and the entry of new firms, and works to eliminate abnormal profits when they occur. Without profit maximization as an assumption, many predictions of our theory would become discouragingly fuzzy.

For over a century, economists accepted the idea that firms do want to maximize profits. Their arguments seemed strong. Perfectly competitive and monopolistically competitive firms had to maximize profits, for any deviation from the profit maximum automatically meant losses. (In both market cases, competition ensures that in the long run only normal profit is being earned. Any reduction in that means losses.) An oligopolist or a monopolist with more market power has greater leeway, but even then profit maximization seems logical. If management decides not to do so, and seeks some other goal (a quiet life or community service, for example), it is likely to find itself in hot water with its stockholders. Other firms which do earn higher profits will be held up for unfavorable comparison at the annual meeting. Managers will thus be prodded toward profit maximization even when they are otherwise inclined.

Over the years several objections have been made against the assumption; these deserve some discussion.

1. It is often said that firms do not possess completely the data needed to construct the cost and revenue curves of our analysis. In fact, many businessmen have never even *seen* the diagrams used in this book. How then can the theory be correct? Though this objection sounds serious, it involves a fundamental error of logic. The theory predicts only that firms will behave in a certain way: maximizing profits. Such behavior may come about via trial and error, or careful judgment, or luck—or by using our theoretical tools.

2. Other factors besides profit clearly motivate a firm. Large sums may be spent to foster good will in the community. Firms may avoid handling profitable goods because of the calumny attached to them (some theatres will not show X-rated films, some manufacturers would not produce napalm). The last penny of profit may not be squeezed out of the consumer because federal antitrust action is feared. Similarly, the profit maximum may be avoided so as not to attract the competition of newcomers to the industry, and to avoid stimulating high wage demands from labor unions. All these examples of behavior are common. Yet the believer in profit maximization sees a pattern developing as these examples are quoted. Pro-

mote good will, avoid unpopularity, stay clear of the antitrust laws, restrict the competition, and restrain labor unions. Note what they all have in common. Contrary policies are likely to have a negative effect on the firm's profits over time. The behavior described here may be nothing more than *profit maximization in the long run.* Unfortunately, it is often difficult to decide whether settling for less immediate profit is a real deviation from our theory, or whether it is a case of long-run maximization.

3. William J. Baumol of Princeton University has advanced an ingenious alternative to the theory in its specialized application to oligopolies.[7] Baumol believes that the aim of the large oligopolistic firm, although it may originally have been profit maximization, has changed over time. Recall the prediction that price and quantity will be difficult to set because of mutual interdependence. But, says Baumol, our theories of the kinked demand curve and tools such as game theory may be too sophisticated for day-to-day decision-making. Many steps are taken which ignore the reaction of other firms. Important judgments such as inventory size, transport patterns, additions to and removals from the list of products marketed, and research seldom include projections of rivals' countermoves.

How can this be so? Baumol argues that ordinary decisions of a firm do not normally generate "prompt aggressive countermoves" from competitors because the modern giant corporation is enormously complex, thus often clumsy and slow-moving. If one firm makes a move which is not too radical, that move may be ignored by competitors. Even if steps are taken, they will involve lengthy discussions in committee meetings and a long time lapse before they become effective. Further, says Baumol, the management of many firms may be too busy and their skills too limited to use complicated formulae for profit maximization. Hence they use rules of thumb, such as setting price by adding a standard percentage mark-up on top of costs, and devoting a fixed percentage of total revenue to advertising and research for quality change.

These rules of thumb may originally have implicitly led to profit maximization, but to be useful they must be simple, and to be simple they cannot take explicit account of what other firms do. The result is unlike the orthodox theory. Price cuts

---

[7] *See his* Business Behavior, Value, and Growth *(New York: Harcourt Brace Jovanovich, 1967).*

may not be matched after all if competing firms are using a system of mark-up pricing too.

Baumol advances an alternate hypothesis to explain the aims of oligopoly. There is some evidence, he says, to show that the size of a firm's operation shares the stage with profit in the role of the firm's prime objective. What is this evidence? First, the bigger the firm the more chance that it will gain advantages in borrowing on the capital market. A very large firm can often get a lower interest rate on its bank loans and bond issues than can a small but highly profitable firm. Even more significant, there appears to be a glitter associated with large size alone. The salaries of middle and top managers appear to be correlated more with sales volume than with profits. More often than not, a vice president in a large but only moderately profitable firm makes much more than the same official of a small and highly profitable enterprise. Baumol notes that the requirements for membership in the Young Presidents Organization include being under 40 and president of a company whose annual sales volume is over a million dollars. It is both significant and amusing that no mention is made of profit. For all we know, the next handsome YPO member we see may be coming from bankruptcy court.

Supporters of Baumol's position would agree that not maximizing profit is different from ignoring it. There must certainly be a minimum "profit constraint"—some level below which profit cannot dip if the stockholders are to be kept satisfied, and if the firm is to earn enough to reinvest in new plant and equipment.

We can see that the question of whether firms do maximize profit or not is complex and difficult to solve. Studies are continuing in this area, and new evidence will mean modifiying the traditional theory in coming years.

Questions

1. Why might firms not maximize short-run profits?
2. What is a plausible substitute for the theory of profit maximization?

9.

PARADISE REGAINED, PART ONE: How Can Market Power Be Controlled?

The past few chapters showed that when market power is exerted by monopolies or oligopolies, society can expect higher prices caused by restricted output, unequal income distribution due to monopoly profits, and stagnant conditions caused by an absence of competition. Offsetting advantages occur as well, in particular the ability to realize economies of scale through mass production, and more debatably to finance research from profits.

Whenever legislatures come to believe that the disadvantages outweigh the potential gains, movements spring up to regulate and restrict market power. Such control can be attempted in several ways. Government can nationalize firms, operating them directly as with most European railways, telephone companies, and the like.[1] Or government can purchase a portion of a firm's common stock. Though this portion may be below 50 percent, the large block of shares will give the authorities a means to supervise and to influence corporate behavior. This is common practice in Sweden. Alternately, the firm with market power can be allowed to continue completely in private hands, but subject to the supervision of government public utility (regulatory) commissions.[2] Finally, the attempt

---

[1] In a subsequent volume the pros and cons of the state-run firm in the Soviet Union will be examined.

[2] Be careful to note that the term "public utility" can cause confusion. In spite of the word public, the utility is privately owned and operated.

may be made to break up firms that have market power into smaller, more competitive units, by enforcing antitrust laws.

PUBLIC UTILITIES

Public utility regulation and antitrust laws are the methods most used in the US, and we will consider them in detail. Public utilities in general must gain government approval for changes in price and output. State governments deal with intrastate business activity, while various federal commissions regulate interstate commerce. Examples of the latter include the Interstate Commerce Commission (I.C.C.) for railroads and trucking, the Civil Aeronautics Board (C.A.B.) for airlines, and the Federal Communications Commission (F.C.C.) for radio and TV broadcasting. Typically, these commissions judge rates by the criterion of the "fair return." The fair return price is one which covers all costs of production including a reasonable profit. This is rarely easy to establish. Many differences of opinion exist between the utility and the regulatory commission as to what constitutes legitimate expenses, and the privately owned utility has a vested interest in inflating its costs.[3]

In recent years there has been a spate of criticism directed against many of the federal regulatory commissions. It is said that their actions have benefited the firms they are supposed to regulate rather than serving the interests of the consuming public. This is a highly charged political question on which easy answers should not be expected.

ANTITRUST LAWS

Antitrust law is equally part of the political arena. In no other area of economics have court decisions played a more important role or been more controversial. Antitrust legislation is remarkably old, considering the high degree of concentration in American industry today. The first such law, the outcome of populist agitation against monopoly behavior in the Midwest,

---

[3] One controversial example much in the news recently involves advertising. Electric power companies have mounted large-scale attacks on environmentalists in the press, and as these ads are included in the utilities' costs, willy-nilly the consuming public pays for them.

was passed in Kansas in 1889; fifteen states had antitrust laws by 1893. State efforts at control were largely doomed from the beginning, however, because of the constitutional prohibitions against interference with interstate commerce. The first federal law in this area was the famous Sherman Antitrust Act of 1890, named for Senator John Sherman of Ohio.[4] Nothing in his career suggested that he would be the man to lead an anti-monopoly crusade; indeed, his bill was loosely worded and full of loopholes. Combination or conspiracy in restraint of trade or commerce is illegal, said the act, but there was a critical failure to define these terms adequately. The Sherman Act also suffered from lack of an enforcement agency (the Antitrust Division of the Justice Department was not established until 1903), and from a hostile Supreme Court. The Court's 1895 ruling in *U.S.* v. *E. C. Knight Co.* that "commerce is not manufacture," illogical as that seems today, emasculated the act for years with regard to manufacturing.

The man whose name no one can pronounce changed all that. A 32–caliber bullet from the revolver of Leon Czolgosz killed President William McKinley in 1902 and thrust Theodore Roosevelt into the White House. Over the years more and more Roosevelt-appointed members joined the Supreme Court. In the Northern Securities Co. case of 1904, by a close 5–4 vote, the act was rejuvenated. The Northern Securities Co., in spite of its innocent title, was a cover to merge the railway empires controlled by E. H. Harriman, J. P. Morgan, and James J. Hill, which would have put four of the six transcontinental railroads under the same management. In the next year, 1905, the case of *Swift and Co* v. *U.S.* broke up the beef monopoly at the very time that Upton Sinclair's famous book, *The Jungle,* so outraged the consuming public that the Pure Food and Drug Act was rushed through Congress (1906).[5]

The most famous year for the "trust-busters" was without doubt 1911, when the Supreme Court broke up John D.

---

[4] *Sherman was the younger brother of General William Tecumseh Sherman of Civil War fame; he was twice a candidate for the Republican presidential nomination, and served as both Secretary of State and Secretary of the Treasury. Sherman was a key man in the wheeling and dealing of 1876, when the presidency was virtually stolen from Samuel Tilden and given to Rutherford B. Hayes.*

[5] *The Jungle, with its lurid tales of filth and rats surrounding (and even included in) the products of the meat packing industry, remains the best polemic novel on the days when monopolies rode roughshod over the consumer. The book still evokes revulsion against the trust system.*

Rockefeller's huge Standard Oil Company,[6] and forced the reorganization of the tobacco trust in *U.S. v. American Tobacco Company.* But there was a catch to these heady victories. The Court concluded that some monopolies were worse than others, holding in these cases that only undue or unreasonable restraint of trade was illegal under the Sherman Act. This so-called "rule of reason" was confirmed in 1920, when the Court refused to convict J. P. Morgan's great combine, the U.S. Steel Co., even though it controlled nearly 60 percent of the industry and had potential monopoly power. It is not enough to show bigness, held the Court. It declared that "the law does not make mere size an offense. It . . . requires overt acts." Furthermore, the Court continued, no law was broken, even though management had intended to monopolize the market, and had conspired to fix prices. But the Justices believed that very attempt proved that there was no actual monopoly power, for if there were, there would be no need for price fixing agreements—a sample of judicial logic that is about as convincing today as the Dred Scott Decision. The Court backed this up in 1927 (*U.S. v. International Harvester*), declaring that there is no crime "however impressive is the existence of unexerted power." The rule of reason seriously hindered antitrust prosecution for many years to come.

Meanwhile, in 1914, Woodrow Wilson's administration shepherded through Congress the Clayton Antitrust Act which strengthened the Sherman Act in four main areas. The Clayton Act outlawed price discrimination that tended to create monopoly (as when producers give cut rates to each other to undercut and eliminate competitors). The Act also made illegal tied contracts in which the contracting parties agree not to buy or sell the products of competitors. The acquisition of stockholding in competing companies was prohibited where this tends to lessen competition.[7] Interlocking directorates (one or more individuals serving simultaneously on the boards of different firms) were forbidden where the firms are in competition. Finally, corporate officials can be held personally responsible for monopoly practices. Under the Sherman Act, only the

---

[6] *Today existing as several independent companies including Standard Oil of New Jersey (Exxon), Standard Oil of New York, Standard Oil of Ohio, Standard Oil of Indiana, and Standard Oil of California.*

[7] *This clause was used to force DuPont to divest itself of its large holdings of General Motors stock in 1957.*

corporation, and not its managers, could be penalized following conviction. The Clayton Act was the statute under which several G.E. and Westinghouse officials were sentenced to prison for price fixing in 1961.[8] The Clayton Act was buttressed by the companion Federal Trade Commission Act of 1914. The F.T.C. was set up to consider complaints, especially of unfair competitive practices including false advertising. The agency had a powerful weapon in the first five years of its life—the ability to issue "cease and desist" orders without being subject to judicial review, but this was overturned by court decision in 1919. Many observers have mixed feelings about this. The long delays involved in judicial review can allow exploitative practices to continue unchecked for months; on the other hand, the unhindered use of cease and desist is no doubt open to abuse.

During the Great Depression of the 1930s, Congress went through a curious period when it discouraged competition through a number of laws. The short-lived National Recovery Administration, with its public works projects and its famous blue eagle for a symbol, established so-called fair competition codes under which businessmen agreed to avoid price cutting. In some cases, they were encouraged to *raise* prices by cutting output. These codes were enforceable by law, they were exempt from antitrust action, and they affected 500 industries with 22 million workers. Fair competition codes were declared unconstitutional in *Schechter Poultry Corp.* v. *U.S.* (1935), worth remembering if only because the poultry firm's victory over the N.R.A. eagle led this to be known as the "plucked chicken case."

Though the N.R.A. is long gone and nearly forgotten, two pieces of legislation that passed in the aftermath of its demise shared its anti-competitive principles, and still survive.

The Robinson-Patman Act of 1936 was aimed particularly at chain grocery and drug stores. Local stores were being seriously undercut by the chains, which were able because of their size to bargain for quantity discounts and lower advertising rates. The Act prohibited such discounts when these were not based on actual cost economies, and even if they did result from cost economies, it gave the F.T.C. the power to limit them

---

[8] *As will be discussed in chapter 13, one other important provision of the Clayton Act is the exclusion of labor unions from its antitrust provisions.*

when they are "unjustly discriminatory." Similarly, the sale of goods at "unreasonably low prices" was prohibited. Evidence shows that one result has been a curtailment of price competition in retail markets. Some small and inefficient sellers which would otherwise not be able to compete have thus continued in operation.

The Robinson-Patman Act was followed in 1937 by the Miller-Tydings Act, which passed into law as a rider to a District of Columbia financial bill.[9] The Miller-Tydings Act legalized the system of resale price maintenance (R.P.M.) which applies at present to about half the states of the union. Sellers of nationally-known brand-name merchandise, and their influential supporters in various trade organizations, were the chief lobbyists for R.P.M. The system of R.P.M. works as follows: a state is permitted to opt for R.P.M. by passing a "Fair Trade Law."[10] Having done so, a manufacturer can then negotiate an agreement with a retailer in that state not to cut prices on his brand-name products. By a feat of legal legerdemain, the contract with one retailer then automatically applies to all sellers in the state (the "non-signer clause"). Many economists look askance at these fair trade laws, believing that they have seriously reduced price competition in the states where they apply. Campaigns to abolish them are common nowadays, and several state legislatures have repealed theirs.

A turnaround toward more energetic use of the antitrust laws had already taken place just before World War II, culminating in the famous Alcoa Case of 1945. In this case, Justice Learned Hand overturned the "rule of reason," holding that overwhelming market power is necessarily an offense.[11]

A year later, in 1946, the Supreme Court took a great step forward in attacking oligopoly. Direct price fixing agreements had always been held illegal under the Sherman Act. However, conviction had not been obtained where firms behaved as if they were fixing prices, but no agreement could be proven to

---

[9] Neither the first nor the last time an important bill in economics has slipped through Congress tacked on to some humdrum revenue measure.

[10] Another example of good public relations in choosing names. It takes a strong will, does it not, to oppose anything so reasonable as "fair trade."

[11] Though the Supreme Court for some years seemed to back away from the straightforward decision in the Alcoa Case, its basic logic was reaffirmed in U.S. v. Grinnell Corporation (1966), where a company dealing in fire sprinklers was convicted on the theory that monopoly power alone is illegal.

exist. In *American Tobacco Co.* v. *U.S.* (1946) the Court cut through this knot by finding that agreement could be inferred. The three major US tobacco companies, American, Liggett and Myers, and R. J. Reynolds, priced their products and paid tobacco growers so similarly that price fixing could be deduced. The future thus seemed bright for the prosecution of oligopolistic behavior. However, more recent court decisions have not sustained this promise, and for the moment the direct frontal assault on oligopoly has lost force.

Congress passed an important measure in 1950 to fill a gaping loophole in the Clayton Act. Under the latter, acquiring ownership of a competing firm could clearly be illegal. But a 1926 decision, *Thatcher Manufacturing Co.* v. *F.T.C.*, held that the merger of companies via the acquisition of assets was quite all right. The Clayton Act could not therefore be used to prevent mergers. The Celler-Kefauver Act (1950) declared illegal any acquisition or merger which "substantially lessens competition or tends to create a monopoly." Recent uses of the Act range all the way from forbidding the amalgamation of Bethlehem Steel and the Youngstown Sheet and Tube Corporation (1958), to preventing the merger of two food store chains in Los Angeles (*U.S.* v. *Von's Grocery*, 1966). Both horizontal mergers between sellers of the same good, and vertical mergers between a producer and a user of some input (iron ore, coal, and steel, for example) have been prosecuted under Celler-Kefauver in recent years.

A third type of merger—the conglomerate, where the firms involved neither supply nor compete with one another—has been a puzzle for antitrust lawyers. Under what conditions do conglomerate mergers lessen competition? This question is far from fully answered at present, but one recent case shows one area, advertising, where the court will draw the line. *F.T.C.* v. *Procter and Gamble* (1967) resulted from the purchase by Procter and Gamble in 1957 of the bleach producer, Clorox, for $30 million. Mr. Justice William Douglas, speaking for a unanimous court, pointed to Procter and Gamble's "huge advertising advantages" which might lessen competition in the bleach industry. Procter and Gamble's ad budget was in excess of Clorox's total sales; "it can and does feature several products in its promotions," thus reducing the unit costs of advertising. The Court's decision continued that "it also purchases network programs on behalf of several products, enabling it to give each product network exposure at a fraction of the cost per product that a firm with only one product to advertise would incur."

Another recent case shows that the Court will allow a merger if a big conglomerate on the outside of an industry looking in acquires a smaller firm and thus gains a toehold in the industry (*F.T.C.* v. *the Bendix Corporation*, 1970).

One final area of antitrust law has been debated inconclusively for many years. Taking out a federal patent on some exceptional new invention or process is a perfectly legal way to obtain and to keep market power (some examples were given on page 85). It is immediately apparent that a conflict of public interests exists. Most people would agree that inventors should be rewarded for their time and effort, but these same people also agree that monopoly power should be controlled to protect the consumer. What is to be recommended? Compromise solutions are easy enough to conjure up. One of the most appealing is to require the holder of a patent to license it to any user willing to pay a fixed percentage of the profits earned from its use. But this represents a major change in current law, which allows a patent holder to be very restrictive in using his invention. In fact, he does not have to use it at all if he so chooses! In *Hartford-Empire Co.* v. *U.S.* (1945), the principle was established that holders of patents may suppress entirely the use of their discoveries for the 17–year period.[12] Patent holders also have the right to place severe conditions on license holders who pay for the privilege of using a patent. In spite of this, in recent years the Supreme Court has begun to attack monopoly practices when they involve patent arrangements. For example, some cross-licensing whereby firms share patents with one another to gain a market advantage has been declared illegal. But the big problem concerning monopoly founded on one company's control of patents and subsequent research remains unsolved.

What should we conclude about the present state of antitrust laws? Have they retarded the growth of market power or rolled back that power? It seems apparent that in a goodly number of important instances the spread of monopoly has been hindered. However, for those who believe that government must

---

[12] *This case is an important reason why major technological breakthroughs have sometimes not been adopted by oligopolistic industries. They control the patents. Some companies—United Shoe Machinery, for instance—did a fine job of locking away many patented inventions to forestall competitors from using them.*

bring more effective competition into the market place, the results seem bleak. Numerous studies attest to increasing, not decreasing, concentration in American industry. Oligopoly behavior is the norm for big business, but the authorities have hesitated to undertake any broad frontal attack on the oligopolies. One yardstick of antitrust action which will be noteworthy through the 1970s is treatment of the petroleum industry. When prices were shooting up and independent gasoline dealers were being squeezed out in 1973, demands were heard that more competition be enforced, perhaps by separating retail gas outlets from the parent company. Another measure will be the outcome of the appeal by IBM against a spectacular damage award made to Telex, an Oklahoma corporation. Telex complained against alleged monopoly practices by IBM and sued in federal districtcourt. The case, decided in September, 1973, appears to mark a tendency for competing companies to use lawsuits as a retort to predatory practices. What the higher courts do with this case on appeal, and what happens to the petroleum industry, should be good indications of the path antitrust enforcement will take in the years immediately ahead.

Questions

1. What are the ways in which market power can be controlled?
2. What are the major pieces of antitrust legislation? What are their strengths and weaknesses?
3. What were the major court decisions in the area of antitrust law? What was the economic impact of these decisions?
4. Why are patents a special problem of antitrust enforcement?

10

PARADISE LOST, PART TWO: When Social Costs and Benefits Diverge from Private Costs and Benefits

A capsulized view of the advantages of perfect competition is that society receives maximum benefits because that system pares cost and eliminates abnormal profit, promoting efficient production. The past few chapters have shown how the predictions of perfect competition are interfered with when firms attain market power.

SOCIAL COSTS

There is another broad area where the presumed advantages may not hold. The market system's answers to the great economic questions of what to produce and by what method to produce it are predicated on private decisions by buyers and sellers. Yet most such decisions will have "externalities" —non-market effects on others not directly concerned with the buying or selling. These external consequences are often quite insignificant, as when a jealous person resents (or a generous person applauds) the purchase of a new car by a neighbor. Sometimes, however, the externalities can be extremely important.

Take, for example, the Paul Lewter Lumber and Paper Company of Makesmee, Ill. The Lewter Company has many competitors in its timber and sawmill operations, and has thus weighed carefully its methods of operation to minimize its production costs.[1] However, Mr. Lewter considers as costs only those items that he pays for—his private costs. There are several other costs that do not affect his pocketbook, and hence do not affect his operation. For example, his loggers have stripped the timber from the shores of the Makesmee River, and the increased runoff of rainfall has eroded neighboring farms and flooded property downstream. His mill dumps waste products into the river, and fishermen are never seen on the banks of the Makesmee these days. The stench of sulphur dioxide from the paper-making plant is oppressive on calm days, and the harsh whine of the power saws is heard all night long.

The private cost to Lewter of all this is exactly zero. He need pay not one penny for the air, water, and noise pollution that he is causing. Yet these cause annoyance and real hardship to many residents of Makesmee and its surrounding farms. Such costs are called social costs—not reflected by the private market, but costs all the same.[2] Note that Lewter's decision to treat the environment as a free waste disposal system is quite rational on a private basis. The market system as we know it gives no signal that this private advantage to Lewter is very much less than the social costs he inflicts on the public.

A high official of the US Environmental Protection Agency has said that the divergence between private and social costs is the fundamental cause of all types of pollution. In defense of the market system, there is no reason to expect such a divergence in most economic activity. Decisions based on private cost only are most often quite correct from a social point of view. Even when they are not, if the difference between private and social costs is not very great it may be much better simply to accept the resulting inefficiency than to adopt a scheme of bureaucratic control which may be worse.

---

[1] *Remember our contention that a competitive firm tends to produce at a quantity and price which minimizes costs per unit (shown in chapter 4). We mean by that private costs to the firm.*

[2] *The term "external diseconomies" has the same meaning.*

SOCIAL BENEFITS

Social costs are not the only form of "externality." Sometimes the action of one person or group will have nonmarket beneficial effects on others. One of the earliest examples used in economics was that of the bees and the farmer. When Mr. Bumble's bees swarm from his apiary, they gather on neighbor Ferguson's apple trees, pollinating them and ensuring a large output of fruit, the cider from which will keep Ferguson warm all winter long. Bumble cannot charge for the service—the bees go where they will. But there has been a social benefit (or external economy) to Ferguson greater than the private benefit which Bumble gets from his honey business. Similar logic will show the social benefit from a new railroad or subway line. On a private basis, the benefit to the builders is the revenue they can collect for selling tickets. On a social basis the benefit is much greater. Consider for example the reduced congestion on nearby highways, and the increased property values in communities served by the improved transport facilities.[3] Here too the market system will not signal accurately what should be done to maximize society's (as contrasted to the private entrepreneur's) welfare.

Of other such social benefits, compulsory education is perhaps most important. Schooling to make little John a good citizen instead of an illiterate clod will make life easier in his adulthood for little Chris, who will presumably find better government, less crime, more interesting movies and TV fare, and so forth. Attractive architecture and handsome landscaping are further examples of social benefits.

SOCIAL COSTS AND BENEFITS SHOWN DIAGRAMMATICALLY

What are the economic implications of a difference between private and social costs and benefits? Take social costs first. Figure 10–1 shows the supply and demand for the wood products made by Lewter and other firms in his industry. The supply curve S_P shows the situation when only private costs must be

---

[3] Of course, the new line may have social costs as well—noise, fumes, and perhaps degradation of scenery.

FIGURE 10-1

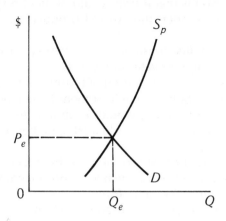

considered by suppliers. Equilibrium price will be OP$_e$, and equilibrium quantity OQ$_e$. However, if Lewter and other firms were responsible for covering the social costs of their production, then for any quantity they would have to be paid a higher price with which they could cover the added costs. See how in Figure 10-2 the supply curve S$_s$, reflecting social costs, lies above S$_p$ all along its length. To supply a quantity OQ$_e$, firms must be paid a higher price OP$_h$. But this is not equilibrium. Neither price nor quantity could stay that high because of competitive pressure, and would settle at OP$_l$ and OQ$_l$ respec-

FIGURE 10-2

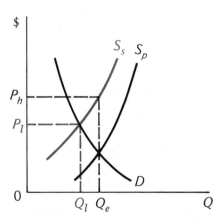

tively. The lesson is that if firms could be held responsible for their social costs, then they would produce less at a higher price.

For social benefits the situation is reversed. Private demand is D_p on Figure 10–3, private supply is S_p. The resulting equilibrium price is OP_e, while the equilibrium quantity is OQ_e. If nonmarket social benefits could somehow be made to accrue to the producing firm, this would result in a growth of supply to S_s. The new equilibrium would lead to higher output OQ_h at a lower price OP_1.

In short, where there are social costs the forces of the private market economy cause too much to be produced. Where there are social benefits, the same forces cause too little to be produced. Unless this situation is adequately measured and corrected, the predicted advantages of perfect competition will be offset to the degree that externalities are important. Measurement and correction are discussed in the following chapter.

An observer might be tempted to say, why not utilize the private market to rectify the externalities? Could not an entrepreneur find a good return in eliminating social costs for people, or in bringing social benefits to the public for profit? The rub here is that private enterprise will not find it easy, for the following two reasons.

FIGURE 10–3

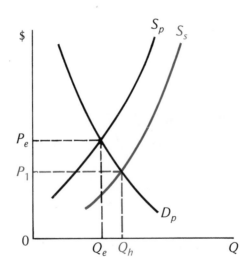

1. Many projects involving the elimination of social costs or the provision of social benefits will not be profitable, because people can see that they will get the advantage of a project even without paying for it. Several examples can demonstrate this point. Say a town's police force is marketed on a subscription basis. You pay an annual fee for protection, just as was the situation in London before 1829.[4] But if the force is well-run, then everyone benefits from the lower crime rate whether they are subscribers or not, and a private protection company finds it hard to attract paying clients. The same is true of defense in general. Defense can certainly be marketed as a product—in medieval times wealthy guild merchants in Italian or Flemish city-states would hire mercenary soldiers. But all residents of the city would be protected by the soldiers manning the walls, even those who did not contribute. Street lights, flood control, urban rapid transit which reduces highway congestion, and the elimination of pollution in general are further cases where the market system does not work well because no one can be excluded from the benefits.[5]

2. The other reason why the private market will not fully solve the social cost/benefit problem concerns areas where it would be undesirable or dangerous to exclude any non-paying individual. Take the fire department as a good example. In the 18th and 19th centuries, private fire fighting companies were common in both Britain and America. Subscribers hung the appropriate company medallion on their walls for identification. The problem was that fires starting on unprotected premises could become conflagrations that were impossible to stop when they reached a building with paid up fire protection. The possible "externality" of a fire was too great to ignore. Similarly, innoculations, vaccinations, water purification, and the like *can* be done on a private basis, but there is an intolerable risk of epidemics which would be harmful to the fabric of society. Similar logic can be used for hospitals, mental institutions, and schools, although in all three fields private establishments flourish and at least one prominent economist, Milton Friedman, would like to see the private sector predominate in these activities.

---

[4] *Sir Robert Peel established the London Metropolitan Police in that year. The word "bobby" in referring to London policemen comes from his name.*

[5] *This is called the property of "nonexcludability" in the jargon. Those who benefit but will not pay are called "free riders."*

Questions

1. What are social costs? Social benefits?
2. How would market decisions be altered if social costs and social benefits could be taken into account?
3. Why is it not profitable for an entrepreneur to eliminate social costs, or to bring social benefits to people?

11.

PARADISE REGAINED, PART TWO: Narrowing the Gap Between Private and Social Costs and Benefits

In the last chapter, we saw that without help the private market cannot satisfactorily cope with the problems of social costs and benefits. This chapter will explore corrective action that can be taken.

ESTIMATING SOCIAL COSTS

Little success can be anticipated unless a system of measuring externalities is developed. Our abilities to do so are gravely limited by a lack of suitable techniques. Both in theory and in day-to-day planning one of the greatest difficulties in modern economics is assessing social costs and benefits. Only a small proportion of these externalities can be measured easily.

To use our old example of the Lewter Company in Makesmee, Ill., studies could show some direct costs imposed by pollution: houses have to be painted every three years instead of every ten, fabrics wear out sooner because of the more frequent laundering they need, commercial fishermen no longer fish the Makesmee River and the Makesmee water works has to use special filters in its purification plant.[1] In

---

[1] It has been estimated that pollution in New York City raises the costs of painting, washing, laundry, and the like by $200 per person per year.

addition there are other costs which may be just as onerous for the community, but which are much harder to estimate. What is the dollar value of not being able to swim or boat in the Makesmee River, of the noise from the Lewter plant, of the fumes and congestion caused by trucks coming and going, of the haze which blots out the stars at night, of the reduced wildlife population in the area, of the industrial odors and the stinging eyes? We are sure these are costs, but how large are they?

Several methods of estimation have been suggested. Comparisons could be made of property values in polluted Makesmee with similar properties in similar communities without pollution. The differential might approximate the social costs involved. Another method would be to ask citizens how much they would pay to eliminate one type of pollution.

Answers to the "air pollution questionnaire" will differ depending on personal views, ranging perhaps from Preacher Longstaff's $200 through banker Brown's $100, teacher Stafford's $75, and Mr. Lewter's zero (he thinks the plant smells fine). For these four individuals, total social costs are $375; following the same idea for the whole town, we would know how much to shift the supply curve in Figure 10–2 to reflect social costs.

The major problem with such surveys is how to be certain that people tell the truth. People might think that they will be charged for pollution control in proportion to their answers, thus leading to very low estimates. Or they may think that the highest social cost will be tackled first by the federal government, causing inflated estimates to be given. One possible approach is an independent survey of the type done recently by the respected *Economist* magazine of London. A hypothetical sum of money (say $1,000) is assigned to each voter, who is instructed to allocate it on a form sheet among many possible programs to eliminate social costs or realize social benefits. The principle of a fixed sum to be allocated avoids both under-estimation or inflation of the totals. Some authorities feel that surveys of this type may be the best approach to estimating the dollar value of externalities. Care would have to be used however, because polluting firms with large advertising budgets might have a substantial advantage over conservation groups in attracting and holding public attention. The results of the survey might be influenced accordingly.

DEALING WITH SOCIAL COSTS
AND BENEFITS

Once the difficulties of measurement are overcome, the next question is what to do with the figures obtained. How to adjust the private market to take account of social costs and benefits is one of today's most significant economic problems. The most common solution is government regulation. The government prohibits some things (such as very high compression engines, factory smoke emissions, submachine guns) and makes mandatory other things (such as no-start seat belt devices, catalytic converters, compulsory public education). Clearly, government regulation of this type will always be necessary; for example, no alternate arrangement can beat strict prohibition as a way to keep submachine guns out of careless hands. However, such regulation is managed by a bureaucracy. Traditionally, bureaucracies are cumbersome and slow-moving, often lacking in both energy and imagination. The information available to the government may be inadequate, the regulation likely to be blunt. To avoid undue complication, standards tend to be overly uniform (exhaust emissions which contribute to heavy pollution in downtown Los Angeles are not noticed on the road in northern Maine). Worse yet, a set standard gives no incentive for improvement to the company being regulated. A law requiring a 25 percent reduction of waste disposal into the Makesmee River can be satisfied by just that; firms need not search for ways to improve on this showing.

Because of these difficulties, many economists favor using the economic tools of tax and subsidy to cope with externalities. In the US, a tax on social costs (called an "effluent charge" where pollution is concerned) is the most popular suggestion at present. If a tax were established per unit of pollution, note the advantages. Firms willing to supply the quantities shown along the supply curve of Figure 11–1 would now be willing to supply those amounts only if they are paid the former price plus the amount of the tax (shown here as equal to AB). The supply curve shifts back to S_t, giving a new equilibrium with less output (OQ_t instead of OQ_e—just what the doctor ordered to deal with social costs). Further, government need not engage in specialized research to determine how to cut pollution. The firms which should be most knowl-

FIGURE 11–1

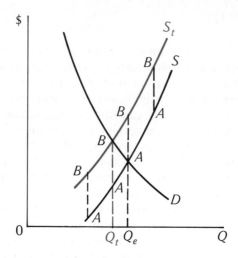

edgeable about their own operations anyway now have a financial incentive to search for the most efficient form of pollution control. Joint projects realizing economies of scale may well result. At present we require the same exhaust devices on the limousine which gets 6 miles to a gallon as the small import which gets 30. A tax per unit of emission would have the effect of making it more expensive to run the big car, shifting new car sales toward the smaller car. The tax can be adjusted up and down depending on its success or lack of it in controlling pollution. In spite of these advantages, however, government regulation is presently much more common than using the tax mechanism in controlling social costs.[2]

The subsidy mechanism can be used when production carries social benefits. Unfortunately, subsidies in the US have too often been associated with questionable programs, and thus have a bit of a bad name at present. Administrative and congressional support of subsidies for dairy interests and airlines at the same time these industries were making big political contributions, huge cost overruns which had to be made up on the Lockheed C5A, Grumman F-111, and the "Spruance" (DD963) class destroyers being built by Litton Industries, have left many observers jaundiced. But subsidies do promote more output, as seen in Figure 11–2. Firms willing to supply various

---

[2] *With one major exception—liquor taxes, where one purpose of the steep tax is to limit consumption of alcohol.*

FIGURE 11–2

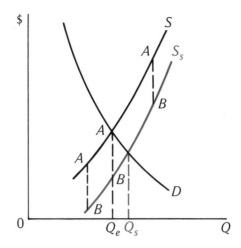

quantities at market prices shown along the supply curve will be willing to supply the same quantities at a lower price when a subsidy is paid. If the dollar value of the grant is equal to AB, then a new supply curve S_s would result, and the new equilibrium shows that a greater quantity will be produced (OQ_s rather than OQ_e). Undoubtedly, subsidies can be used to encourage production that carries social benefits.

Thus we see that several techniques are available for rectifying the deviation between private and social costs and benefits. Coming years are sure to see many developments in this area, one of the most critical problems which traditional economics has failed to solve.

Questions

1. What are the possibilities for measuring social costs and benefits?
2. Why is the accurate estimation of these costs and benefits so difficult?
3. What are the pros and cons of using government regulation to narrow the gap between private and social costs and benefits? Of using the tax mechanism?

III.

HOW INCOMES ARE DETERMINED IN THE MARKET SYSTEM

12.

PRODUCTIVITY AND INCOMES

For many chapters now we have been discussing in detail how the market system answers two of the basic questions of economics: what to produce and by what method to produce it. Now we will examine how output, once produced, is distributed for consumption among the members of society. We saw briefly in chapter 1 that the rewards are allocated in a market system to those who own or control the factors of production. These may include land, the return from which is called rent; labor earning wages and salaries; capital on which interest is earned; and entrepreneurship, the return from which is profit. Individuals who possess scarce factors, or factors much in demand by businessmen, will find their income (wages, rent, etc.) higher than for those whose factors are abundant or not much in demand.

You will note that this is another way of saying that the return to the factors of production—the distribution of income—is established by the forces of supply and demand. Fortunately, this means that most of our analytical work is already done, because it mirrors the theory of how products get priced in a market system.

Let us review in detail how the income of any factor is determined in an economy. Figure 12–1 shows supply and demand curves for a particular grade of labor in one industry. (We could equally have chosen land, capital, or entrepreneurship.) Supply slopes upward under the reasonable assumption that paying higher wages will attract more labor to the industry. Demand, sloping downward, calls for more explanation. A big difference between demand for the services of a factor and demand for a product is that the latter is wanted in its own right for consumption. The demand for factors, on the other hand, derives from another cause—the desire to produce and sell

FIGURE 12-1

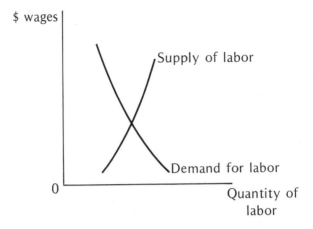

something for profit. The term "derived demand" is used to describe this situation.

Within an industry, what will determine a firm's demand for factors? The firm which is a profit maximizer will want to hire just that quantity of each factor, in just that mix, which will allow it to earn the greatest possible profit. The firm can find these answers by using the profit maximization diagram we are familiar with by now, but which is modified to apply to factor markets.

First the firm will want to know how much revenue will be earned by hiring more and more units of one factor. Once again we use labor as an example. To understand the contribution of labor alone, assume for the moment that the other factors are fixed in quantity: so many acres of land, so many machines and buildings, and so forth. Table 12-1 shows in the

TABLE 12-1

Units of Variable Factor (Labor) Added to Fixed Factors	Total Physical Product (TPP)	Selling Price of Product (P)	Total Revenue Product (TRP)
0	0	$2	$ 0
1	10	2	20
2	25	2	50
3	42	2	84
4	57	2	114
5	64	2	128
6	59	2	108

first column various quantities of labor which could be added by a businessman and used along with the fixed quantities of land, capital, and entrepreneurship. The firm could hire no labor, or it could hire any number up to six. To make its hiring decisions, the firm must know how much output will be forthcoming from the various quantities of labor. The second column shows that there won't be any output at all if no workers are hired, but that output will mount as labor is added. Notice especially that total physical product climbs rapidly at first, then increases more slowly, and even declines when the firm adds a sixth worker (seen at a glance in Figure 12–2). Our data thus obeys a very familiar economic rule: increasing and then diminishing returns to a factor of production. The increasing returns are doubtless due to the more effective division of labor that can be accomplished with more workers. The eventual decreasing returns also make sense because at some point there will be too many workers for the available capital, and there will be overcrowding of the land as laborers get in each others' way. In fact, one of the most consistent phenomena in all economics is this idea of diminishing returns as any variable factor is added to a fixed quantity of other factors. Note how this ties in with our earlier discussion of a firm's short-run costs. The increasing returns when using small amounts of the variable factor help to explain why total costs may rise slowly at relatively low levels of output. Conversely, the decreasing returns which go along with intense factor use help to explain the rapid increase in total costs at relatively high levels of output.

FIGURE 12–2

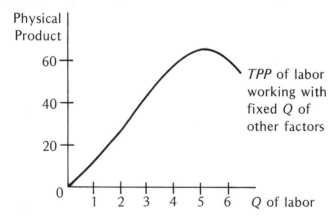

The businessman, however, will find this information on total physical product too limited. He wants to know the profits he can earn by hiring more units of a factor, not just the amount of new output that will result. To find this, he will need to know at what price he can sell the new output. If the firm is in a perfectly competitive industry, then, other things equal, the market price will be constant. Assume, as in column three of Table 12–1, that the market price is $2 per unit. On his calculator the businessman will now be able to multiply the physical product times the price at which the product can be sold. The resulting dollar amount shows various revenues earned by employing varying quantities of labor, and is called *total revenue product* (TRP). Algebraically, TPP × P = TRP. Not surprisingly, since we have multiplied TPP by a constant, TRP shows the same increasing and then diminishing returns, as seen in Figure 12–3.

With this TRP data available, the businessman now needs only one further bit of information to make a rational decision: the cost of hiring men. Assume wages are $20 per man per day. The total factor cost of labor (TCF) will thus be $20 × 1 = $20 for one man, $20 × 2 = $40 for two men, and so forth up to $20 × 6 = $120 for six men. These costs are plotted on Figure 12–4 as a straight line.

To find the optimum quantity of labor to hire, the business-man can now juxtapose the TRP curve of Figure 12–3 and the TCF curve of Figure 12–4; the result is Figure 12–5. Which size labor force maximizes profits? Clearly four men, as at that

FIGURE 12–3

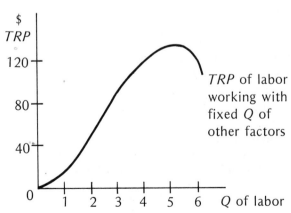

TRP of labor working with fixed Q of other factors

FIGURE 12–4

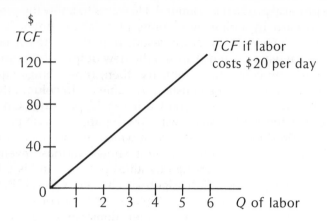

point the total revenue earned from hiring labor exceeds the total cost by the greatest amount, AB.[1] Algebraically, TRP − TCF = total profits from using a factor.

The decision to hire four men is subject to change if any of the underlying conditions are altered. Note the following:

1. If the productivity of labor improves (more physical output per unit of input) then the whole TRP curve will be shifted upward.

2. If the market price at which the final product is sold rises, then the TRP curve will again be shifted upward.

3. If labor costs rise, the TCF line will rise at a steeper slope.

In each case, the point of maximum profit may change, leading to a new decision as to what quantity of a factor to hire.

The framework presented here allows a firm to determine its demand for the factors of production. It is the means by which the firm's demand curve for one factor, labor, shown on Figure 12–1, was first drawn. We can therefore see that the firm's derived demand curve for factors is based on the revenue product that these factors will yield.

All this has not yet told us how the market price (wage) for labor, which we set at $20 per day, was established in the first place. But the tools are already in hand to determine this. The

---

[1] As usual, this point is easily identified by finding where the slopes of the two lines are parallel.

FIGURE 12–5

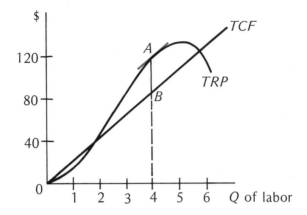

market wage for a certain grade of labor is established by the forces of supply and demand, just as is the price of any other item in the economy.

The supply curve of a factor is usually thought to be upward sloping (Figure 12–6) indicating that higher wages, rent, and so forth, attract greater quantities of a factor into use. The demand curve for a whole market is now easy to find. Each individual firm's demand is determined by the techniques just described. For the total market, these can be summed up by adding them horizontally (a method already used to determine total demand for a product). As seen on Figure 12–7, the equilibrium between supply and demand is at $20, and that is why we used this figure in our original example.-

FIGURE 12–6

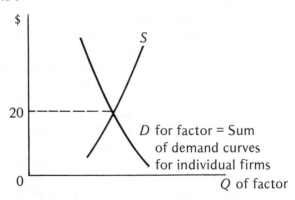

FIGURE 12–7

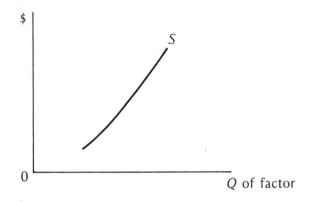

THE ADVANTAGES AND DISADVANTAGES
OF PERFECT COMPETITION
IN FACTOR MARKETS

The mechanism we have just described is exceedingly flexible, just as is the market mechanism for distributing products. Rewards are high or low as supply and demand dictate. When a factor is employed in an area or occupation where the supply of that factor is abundant, or the demand for it is limited, then its income will be low. That factor will then have an incentive to move to an area or industry where incomes are higher. In good measure, this explains why blacks moved in great numbers from the deep South to northern cities, why immigrants came to the New World, why many students go to college, and why farm land close to cities is being sold for development—all without central direction or control. The mechanism is also a regulating device. As factor prices are pushed toward an equilibrium between supply and demand, so shortages and surpluses of any factor are eliminated. For the historian, the reason for the sharp wage increase in 14th century Europe now becomes clear (bubonic plague reduced labor supply). The geologist now sees why his discovery of an ytterbium deposit (Yb, atomic number 70) did not make him rich—the element ytterbium has no known uses, and although supply is low, demand is even lower. The craftsman skilled in making harnesses for horses, the bookkeeper replaced by a computer, the aerospace worker in Seattle, all now see that they have something in common: declining demand for their services, hence lower incomes. In short, a host of problems in many disciplines become explicable when the theory of supply and demand in factor markets is understood.

Economics students may rightly ask themselves, "Is this system fair?" Is it fair that a farmer in Maine does back-breaking work in the rocky soil for low returns, while a lazy land-owner in Oklahoma sips Southern Comfort while the oil royalties flow in? Is it fair that economists are better paid than English teachers, that Elizabeth Taylor makes more in one bad film than a manual laborer makes in a lifetime, that Ali or Frazer get $2½ million each for two months' training and 45 minutes work while in small towns everywhere pugilists battle for $100 a fight? Or fair that the Beatles made more profit from one record than a great symphony orchestra earns in a decade?

The very questions themselves indicate that factor rewards, whether high or low, are in our economic system divorced from any abstract concept of usefulness or fairness. Rewards are high or low because of supply and demand.

At any given point of time, then, we should expect a market system to foster a large degree of income inequality. This is certainly true of the US in spite of numerous public programs (social security, unemployment benefits, welfare, OEO grants, and the like) which transfer funds to low-income groups. As of 1970, the lowest fifth of income recipients, those families earning under $4,000, received only 5 percent of America's total income. The second fifth (income $4,000–7,000) took home 11 percent, the third fifth ($7,000–10,045) received 16 percent, the fourth fifth ($10,045–15,000) earned 24 percent, while the highest fifth of income recipients, with incomes over $15,000, garnered a full 44 percent of all income received.[2]

The word "inequality" conceals real poverty in some areas of the country. Following federal guidelines which define the poverty level as income of less than $4,000 for an urban family of four, 25.5 million Americans, 12.6 percent of the population, were living in poverty. Within this group, 70.1 percent are under 25 or over 65, and 69 percent are white. (Note how the last of these percentages explodes a common myth.) The reasons for long-term poverty are deep, involving lack of education and training, race prejudice, family disintegration,

---

[2] *Wealth, as opposed to income, is even more unequal. Recent statistics show the bottom fifth owned only 7 percent of the nation's wealth, while the share of the top fifth was a little over 60 percent. Huge disparities in stock ownership are a major contributor to wealth inequality.*

cultural deprivation, and many other social and institutional factors. There is widespread agreement that the US is not coping adequately with the problems of poverty. The "welfare mess," so much in the news early in the Nixon Administration, is still a mess. Intriguing suggestions, such as Daniel Patrick Moynihan's for a guaranteed annual income and Milton Friedman's for a negative income tax, have attracted wide attention but have not been adopted.[3] This is depressing for those people who feel that the market system of income distribution, with all its desirable flexibility and economy of operation, will be maintained only if social harmony is preserved. Social harmony is a delicate fabric easily torn. Treating the poor and underpriviliged with compassion, an idea often held grudgingly or viewed with outright hostility in our country, is more than a civil and moral obligation: it is also a useful insurance policy for society.

Questions

1. What determines the income of any factor of production?
2. What will cause a businessman to change his decisions as to how much of a factor he should hire?
3. Are there advantages from a system of perfect competition in factor markets? Disadvantages?

---

[3] The original Nixon-Moynihan Plan of 1969 would have ended the welfare mothers' (AFDC) program under which in most states a family receives no benefits if the father remains at home. Instead, a basic guaranteed income would have been established at $1,600 per year for a family of four. The first $60 per month a family could earn for itself would not count against the $1,600 allowance. Any outside income above $60 per month would reduce benefits by 50¢ on every dollar earned. Thus welfare payments would end when private income reached $3,920. The incentive for the father to disappear would thus be tempered, and welfare payments in the poorer states would be much increased (by over threefold in Mississippi, for example). No part of the plan was more controversial than the work requirement, under which all recipients of aid except mothers with pre-school children must accept either a "suitable" job or job training. The penalty for noncompliance was to be the forfeiture of benefits for the head of household. Friedman's proposal would have accomplished a transfer of income to low-income citizens by building rebates into the federal income tax structure.

APPENDIX

Imperfections and Factor Income: Monopoly, Monopsony, and Bilateral Monopoly

The theory of income distribution discussed thus far has assumed perfect competition among both producers of output and suppliers of input (the factors of production). In four separate cases, imperfections in the market will alter the predictions of our theory. These are taken up below.

MONOPOLY IN THE PRODUCT MARKET

If a firm hiring factors is a monopoly or otherwise an imperfect competitor, a change must be made in computing its revenue product. A perfectly competitive firm can always sell increasing quantities of output at the same price. However, if a monopoly produces and sells more output, the price it receives must fall. The *physical* product of different quantities of labor will be the same as under competition, but not the revenue product. Table 12–2 shows the situation if 100 competitive firms like the one described in Table 12–1 were combined in a monopoly. Columns one, two, and four have therefore been multiplied by 100. Note the importance of column three, which shows that when monopoly attempts to market increased output, the price it receives must fall.

The total revenue product will thus be composed of two ingredients: the rise in revenue gained from selling more out-

TABLE 12–2

Units of Variable Factor (Labor) Added to Fixed Factors	Total Physical Product (TPP)	Selling Price of Product (P)	Total Revenue Product (TRP = TPP × P)
0	0	$3.00	$0
100	1000	$2.75	$2,750
200	2500	$2.50	$6,250
300	4200	$2.25	$9,450
400	5700	$2.00	$11,400
500	6400	$1.75	$11,200
600	5900	$1.50	$8,850

put, minus the loss in revenue caused by the fall in the product price. See what happens if the firm decides to hire five hundred men instead of four hundred. Four hundred men produce 5700 units which, sold at $2.00 each, give total revenue product of $11,400. If another hundred men are hired, 6400 units will be produced. That makes 700 more items which when sold at the new price of $1.75 each would add 700 × $1.75 = $1,225 to revenue product—except that the price is now down to $1.75 not only for the 700 extra units, but also for the 5700 units originally produced. 25¢ is lost on 5700 items, giving a reduction of 5700 × 25¢ = $1,425 in TRP. Thus we have:

Gain from selling 700 new units @ $1.75   =   +$1,225

Loss from reducing price 25¢ on 5700 units   =   −$1,425

Net change in total revenue product   =   −$ 200

Thus hiring five hundred men instead of four hundred will reduce TRP by $200, to $11,200.

The significance of this is that the TRP curve for a monopoly will start to decline *before* the TRP curve under perfect competition (Figure 12–8). Further, it means that for any given wage

FIGURE 12–8

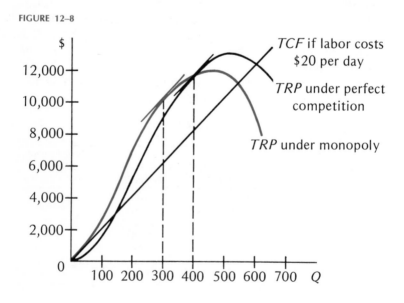

level (such as the $20 per day shown in the figure) a monopoly's profits will be maximized by hiring fewer workers than would be true under perfect competition. Where all the hundred firms in a perfectly competitive industry would find their "profits gap" between TRP and TCF largest for four hundred workers, the monopoly finds its profits maximized by hiring only three hundred workers. This lower demand for factors follows exactly our prediction of chapter 6 that monopolies and other imperfect competitors will find it profitable to restrict their output.

MONOPSONY IN THE FACTOR MARKET

It is possible for the factors of production to suffer from ignorance of alternative uses, or from inability to transfer easily into other occupations.

Under these circumstances a situation of *monopsony* may arise. The Greek *mono opsonein* means single buyer, and a monopsony firm is the only buyer of factors in a particular market.[4] This too will alter the predictions of perfect competition.

Say there is just one employer of labor in an isolated community of northern Michigan, and that the work force there wants to stay put. They may not know of other job opportunities in Illinois or Ohio, they may from tradition or inertia not like to move, or they may simply like life in Michigan. The monopsonistic firm will have a standard demand curve for labor, based on revenue product. The supply curve will be different, however. If it had been a perfectly competitive buyer of factors, the labor market would have been very large in relation to the firm's demand. It would be able to hire any needed quantity at the going market wage rate.[5] However, with no competition for the factors, the firm's supply curve will be that of the whole market, upward sloping as in Figure 12–9. The meaning of this is simple. The firm has been hiring a quantity of labor OQ_1, and has been paying the market wage OW_1. But should it decide to lay off a number of workers Q_1Q_2, then these unemployed workers will cause the market wage to fall to OW_2. Or if it wants to augment its work force by the amount

---

[4] *When a small number of firms are the only buyer, the situation is known as oligopsony.*
[5] *The supply of labor to a perfectly competitive buyer is "perfectly elastic."*

FIGURE 12-9

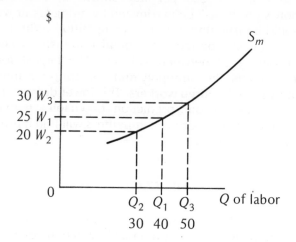

Q₁Q3, then it will have to attract additional labor by paying the higher wage OW3.

This poses a problem of costs for the monopsonist. To get more labor, unlike the competitive firm, it must raise wages for the new workers and also for all the old workers, who must get a raise (they would react poorly to hearing that the newcomers were paid more for the same work). As Figure 12–10 shows, the monopsonist paying $20 per day to hire each of thirty workers ($600 in all) might have to pay $25 per person for 40 ($1,000) or

FIGURE 12-10

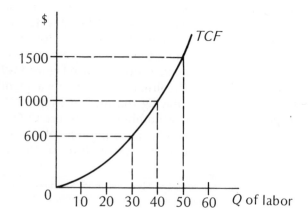

FIGURE 12–11

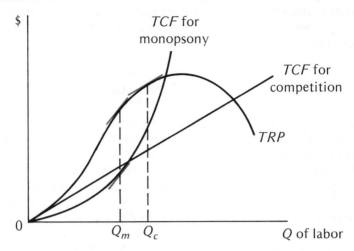

$30 each for 50 ($1,500). In that case, total factor cost will not be a straight line, as it was for a competitive firm, but will slope upward with increasing steepness.

The result is clear when we put this new upward-sloping TCF curve on a diagram with the firm's total revenue product curve (see Figure 12–11). Instead of hiring OQc workers, as would have been done by the firms in a competitive industry, the monopsony will maximize profits by hiring *fewer* workers OQm. This in turn means that the wages paid by the monopsony will be lower than under perfect competition. Figure 12–12 shows that the monopsony would pay OWc were it to

FIGURE 12–12

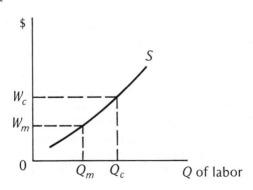

hire OQ_c labor, but having hired the lower quantity OQ_m, it needs to pay only OW_m. To put it bluntly, a monopsony profits by exploiting labor, paying lower wages than would a competitive firm.

MONOPOLY IN THE FACTOR MARKET

Again the predictions of perfect competition will not hold when a seller of factors of production has a monopoly, or substantial market power. Examples might be a well-organized trade union bargaining against many competitive employers, or a powerful land-owners association negotiating with large numbers of tenant farmers for rental contracts. Analytically this is exactly the same as when a monopolist selling output faces many buyers of that output. There is no need to duplicate our previous discussion. A factor monopoly will benefit in the same way as a product monopoly, restricting the use of its "product," charging a higher price for it, and maximizing profits thereby. Some labor unions approximate the conditions of factor monopoly in a market. (Unions are considered in the next chapter.)

FACTOR MONOPOLY AND FACTOR MONOPSONY FACING EACH OTHER: "BILATERAL MONOPOLY"

The term "bilateral monopoly" is the economist's shorthand for the situation comprising a single seller of a factor (factor monopoly) and a single buyer of that factor (factor monopsony). This interesting case is another example of John Kenneth Galbraith's Countervailing Power, a term invented by him to describe the situation when sellers and buyers with market power face each other. It is exemplified by a powerful labor union bargaining against a big corporation. Success comes from strength and skill in bargaining, and the case is as relevant to treaty-making between nations as to equilibrium economics. Economic theory does not allow us to determine what the outcome of the bargains will be, although it does establish the range in which the bargain will lie. The union will aim at its profit-maximizing point, the monopoly price. The big corporation will hope to keep wages much lower than that, maximizing its own profits by paying the monopsonist price. Depending on the strength of the parties and the ability of their negotiators, the bargained wage might be anywhere between the monopolist and the monopsonist solutions. Past agreements between the two, and the pattern of wage settlements in other comparable industries will often carry weight in the bargaining. Aside from this, under bilateral monopoly the wage is indeterminate.[6]

Questions

1. How must the theory of income determination be altered when the buyer of factors is a monopoly? When the buyer is a monopsony? When the seller of factors is a monopoly? When both buyer and seller have substantial market power (bilateral monopoly)?

---

[6] *The mathematical theory of games is a useful tool for analyzing the bargaining positions in bilateral monopoly.*

13.

TOPICS IN INCOME DISTRIBUTION: Unions

The general theory of how income is distributed among the factors of production was the subject of the last chapter. This chapter will examine more closely one topic within that subject—labor unions.

THE RISE OF LABOR UNIONS

The heritage of labor unions, which first sprang up in England, is not so old as might be thought. Labor unions are not related to the medieval craft guilds, whose members often owned capital and employed laborers. In fact, anything resembling a union to raise wages was illegal by British statutes of the 14th and 16th centuries and by the common law as well. By 1800, the Industrial Revolution had created an urban work force, and all combinations of labor were held at law to be criminal conspiracies. As late as 1834, in one of the great turning points of labor history, six workers were arrested for union organizing in an English village with the unlikely name of Tolpuddle. Their conviction as felons and their resulting transportation to Australia caused such a public outcry that the "Tolpuddle Martyrs" were freed, and both courts and parliament took a more lenient stance toward unions.[1]

In the US, early unionizing was local and small-scale (not surprising in a country still basically agricultural) although Americans had their own Tolpuddle experience in 1834 when

---

[1] *In contrast to these early days, British unions today are powerful organizations strongly represented in their own political party (the Labour Party). Their militancy, startling to an American observer, has led to many strikes against the public interest in recent years.*

federal troops were used to put down a canal-construction union which President Andrew Jackson called a riotous assembly. Eight years later, in the pivotal case of *Commonwealth* v. *Hunt* Massachusetts Chief Justice Lemuel Shaw[2] ruled unions and strikes legal and slowly this radical notion became doctrine. An organization known as the Knights of Labor became prominent about 1880. The Knights were an industrial union, the type which attempts to organize all workers, whether unskilled or white collar, under the same wide umbrella. A famous bomb incident at Haymarket Square, Chicago (1886) for which the Knights were blamed, helped to kill that organization but it has modern descendants, the unions grouped in the Congress of Industrial Organization (C.I.O.) founded in 1935. Meanwhile, another type of union was growing in strength during the 1880s. These were the craft unions, limited to practitioners of a particular trade—plumbers, painters, electricians, and the like, united in the American Federation of Labor (A.F.L.) since 1886. The A.F.L. and C.I.O. merged in 1955, but the distinction between industrial and craft unions is as firm as ever.

The progress of American unionism was slow, and tinged with violence. The "Homestead Massacre" of July 6, 1892, though extreme, was too typical of the reaction generated by union organizing efforts. Attempts to unionize the steel industry led to a bitter strike at the Homestead, Pennsylvania, works of the Carnegie Steel Corporation. The strikers armed themselves after learning that the company planned to disperse them with a private army hired from the Pinkerton Detective Agency and equipped with repeating rifles.

The 300 Pinkertons followed a plan worthy of Eisenhower and the Normandy Invasion. They boarded heavily timbered barges and were towed up the Monongahela for an amphibious assault. Striker sentries sighted the barges. No one knows who fired the first shot, but soon there was a regular battle going on. Alas for Pinkerton planners, there had been a cardinal error: The timbers were not thick enough to stop rifle bullets, and the little army floated back downstream defeated, with seven dead and many wounded. Our forefathers in politics and industry could work quickly when they had to. It took just six days to mobilize the state militia, break the strike, and

---

[2] *Father-in-law of Herman Melville and responsible for the first separate-but-equal race decision in 1845.*

put new workers into the mills. There was to be no steel union until the 1920s.

State and federal court injunctions to prohibit strikes before they started became commonplace in the 1890s; that plus the regular army ended the great Pullman Strike of 1894 on the railroads.[3]

A new century and pro-labor Democratic administrations wrought great changes in the status of unions. The first breakthrough was the Clayton Act of 1914, discussed earlier in our chapter on oligopoly. Of great significance, the Act declared that labor is not a commodity or article of commerce, and therefore unions are not liable to prosecution as monopolies in restraint of trade. Under the Roosevelt Administration came a major step forward by unions. The Norris-LaGuardia Act of 1932 eliminated the court injunction as a weapon against strikes, while the Wagner Act of 1935 was more wide-ranging. It outlawed yellow-dog contracts (the ugly-sounding agreement whereby workers could be fired if they joined a union), and prohibited use of threats, force, and other sorts of influence by companies against unions. The most important provision of the Wagner Act guaranteed that a union could become sole bargaining agent by majority vote of the workers in a plant. Elections are supervised by the National Labor Relations Board (N.L.R.B.) which can issue cease and desist orders to stop unfair election practices, and which polices the other sections of the Act.

One era of US labor history was very short-lived. The tactic of seizing plants via a so-called "sit-down strike" gained momentum after a few hundred workers seized the Flint, Michigan, plant of General Motors for 44 days in 1936. Such strikes became common until they were declared illegal in 1939 by the Supreme Court. These were also the years of the last really big-time violence by management against unions. In 1937, the C.I.O. organized the steel industry, but following the precedent of the Homestead battle of 1892, some companies fought it out with firearms. In South Chicago, four were killed and 84 injured by police and vigilantes on Memorial Day, 1937, as the

---

[3] The class antipathy toward organized labor during this period is readily evident from some famous photographs of the Pullman Strike. These photos are highly embarrassing to modern readers with a concern for social justice. One vivid view is of a US Army company drawn up in skirmish line with flags flying, rifles ready, a Gatling gun loaded and aimed, an immaculate officer with drawn sword, all facing what? A shabby, pathetic group of strikers, some clutching boards and clubs, in a vacant lot along a railroad embankment.

Republic Steel Company led the fight against unionization. Senator LaFollette of Wisconsin shocked public opinion with his revelations of Republic's arsenal of small arms, including machine guns, and its organized recruiting of strikebreakers. World War II marked a period of great strength for both the A.F.L. and the C.I.O., but a wave of strikes in 1945 and 1946 led many Congressmen to think that the balance of power was now shifted too far toward the unions. The result was the Taft-Hartley Act of 1947, passed over President Truman's veto.[4] Long and complicated, the Act had three critical provisions.

1. It banned the "closed shop" wherein workers had to be union members to be hired. Unless state law was more restrictive, it permitted the "union shop" under which workers once hired must join the union within a certain time, say 30 days. Finally, by special legislation called "Right to Work" laws, a state could establish the "open shop" where union membership was not necessary to get or to hold a job.[5]

2. A union must give 60-days' notice before striking. If the President of the United States declares a state of emergency, he can ask for a further 80-day "cooling off period" during which a strike is illegal. At the end of the 80 days, the union must vote by secret ballot to approve continuation of the strike. Although it is hard to see exactly why a bargain can be reached during the 80 days which could not be reached during the initial 60, the cooling off period has been a remarkable success. As of the late 1960s, the provision had been used 27 times. All but six disputes were composed during the 80-day period, three of which were settled within a few days thereafter.

3. Unfair labor practices were enumerated and made illegal. Such practices included compulsion of workers to join

---

[4] Thousands of protesters against the Act had massed across from the Capitol on the June day when the veto was overridden. Violence was expected, but did not materialize. Nowadays, unions live rather comfortably with the Act.

[5] A compromise between the union and open shops is the so-called "agency shop." Proponents say it is wrong to force people into a union against their will, and also wrong to give nonunion members a "free ride." (The free ride refers to the fact that if a union, financed by its dues-paying members, wins a wage increase from management, then that increase must apply to all workers, union and nonunion alike.) One solution is to deduct a dollar amount equivalent to dues from the paychecks of nonunion members and hand it over to the union as a fee for services rendered. The agency shop is unpopular. Management doesn't like it because the union will be made financially stronger. Unions, on the other hand, prefer full membership. A group of obscure court decisions has made the agency shop illegal where a state has a right-to-work law.

unions; most jurisdictional strikes (over which unions will represent workers); secondary boycotts (where one union helps another by forcing its employer to boycott the products of another employer); "featherbedding" (work rules which increase the need for labor); and abnormally high dues. The fact that these problems have not all disappeared is due to difficulties of proof before the courts.

It has been fifteen years since the last major piece of labor legislation was passed, the Landrum-Griffin Act of 1959. Aimed at extortion, corruption, and Communist influence in unions, it set new standards for elections, terms and qualifications of union officials, and the administration of union funds.

HOW UNIONS RAISE WAGES

The foregoing discussion has described the legal and historical framework within which unions operate in the modern economy. Now we will analyze the specific methods by which unions attempt to raise wages. Our knowledge of price theory leads us to predict that this can be done either by increasing the demand for labor, by decreasing its supply, or by interfering with the market mechanism through price supports. These three methods are considered below.

1. *Increasing the demand for labor.* Figure 13–1 shows that if a union can somehow stimulate an increased demand for

FIGURE 13–1

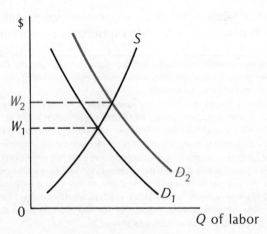

workers among employers (from D_1 to D_2), then market forces will raise wages from the previous level OW_1 to the new, higher level OW_2. How can this be done? Think of what contributes to the demand for labor by a firm. First, its productivity, and second, the price at which the output it produces can be sold. If either of these can be increased, then firms will want more labor, and wages will rise. A union can always try to increase productivity among its members. Exhortations to work harder and more efficiently, plus training and attitude programs are all possibilities. (Although understandably, except during major wars these tactics have had little success in the western world.) The union could also support tariff and quota legislation. Cutting down on foreign competition will tend to keep the demand high for domestic labor. Finally, the union might try to promote featherbedding arrangements with employers. Any work rules which artificially stimulate the need for workers will also increase demand. Some common examples include the requirement of a fireman on diesel locomotives where there is no firebox, the need for a manual typesetter to be present even where type is set electronically, and the necessity for musicians to be present in person even when recorded music is played on stage. Union-set quotas on production can also be established, as when house painters are forbidden to use either brushes over a certain width or rollers (ruled legal in a Supreme Court decision of 1969). Featherbedding is often defended by its supporters as contributing to safety, health, or careful work. All too often, however, it leads to unnecessarily high labor costs and hence to higher prices for the consuming public.

2. *Decreasing the supply of labor.* Shifting the supply curve for labor in an occupation back from S_1 to S_2 will raise wages from OW_1 to OW_2 as shown in Figure 13–2. This can be done by states and by the federal government, as well as by the unions' own rules and regulations. Foreigners can be excluded by strict immigration laws. At both ends of the age spectrum, competing workers can be taken off the market by child labor laws and by compulsory retirement schemes. A shorter work week might be legislated. And government licensing can be encouraged where public safety is involved (plumbers, electricians, cab drivers, etc.). Note that every piece of legislation just mentioned may be socially useful. The neutral observer must realize this, while at the same time appreciating that passage of such laws will economically benefit the unions involved. Politi-

FIGURE 13-2

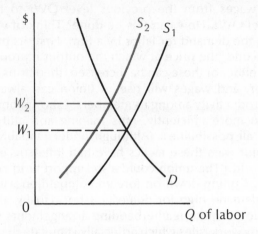

cal action in these areas can thus get a bit contentious. Craft unions can go one step further. If only union men can hold jobs as plumbers, printers, or painters, then labor supply can be limited directly by restricting union membership. Entrance requirements could be made very stiff—very high initiation fees, quotas on new members, exclusive aptitude or intelligence examinations, and perhaps prejudice against blacks, Jews, or other minority groups. Long apprenticeships plus very high annual dues will serve the same end. Even where illegal, enforcement will be difficult and present members will reap the reward of higher wages.

3. *Interfering with the market mechanism through price supports.* Industrial unions of the C.I.O. type, which take in unskilled as well as skilled workers, find it difficult to restrict membership. Rather than shifting the supply curve, they will try to negotiate for their members a wage agreement above equilibrium. Figure 13–3 is analogous to price supports in agriculture. If a union negotiated a wage of OW_u, then those holding jobs would get more pay than if there had been no union—under competitive conditions the wage would have been OW_c. But at the wage OW_u, the employer will not want to hire the competitive quantity of labor OQ_c. He will cut employment along his demand curve to OQ_u, and Q_uQ_c measures the number of workers who are unemployed because of the new wage agreement. The steeper the slope of the demand

FIGURE 13–3

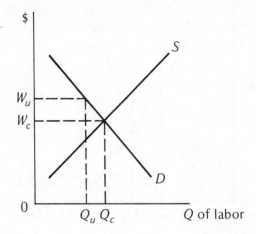

curve, the less unemployment will result and vice versa.[6] Employers will not cut employment much if it is difficult to substitute machines for labor, or if labor is only a small expense of production, or if the higher labor costs can easily be passed on to consumers via price hikes on the product sold.

Even when the resulting reduction in employment will be serious, unions still may seek wage increases eagerly. After all, most employers want to maintain a public relations image and appear to have a social conscience. Rather than lay off workers wholesale, they may reduce their labor force slowly, by not hiring new workers and by not replacing old ones who retire or change jobs. At least temporarily, then, employment will be higher than indicated by the firm's demand curve for labor —say, OQ_{u2} instead of OQ_{u1} in Figure 13–4. A union with sufficient bargaining power might even push the firm off its demand curve in the long run. This could happen only if the firm is earning abnormal profits, part of which could be devoted to hiring unwanted labor if the union's bargaining stance is strong enough.

The best example of a union pushing for higher wages at the expense of increasing unemployment is the United Mine Workers. Until a famous 1950 agreement, mine workers suffered from low wages, but thereafter earnings improved until

---

[6] *Recall that this is an elasticity concept, discussed in chapter 2.*

FIGURE 13–4

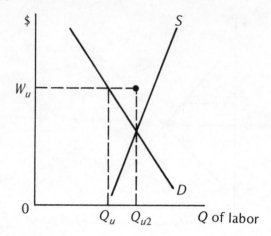

nowadays they are about 25 percent above the national average in manufacturing. However, the high wages stimulated a substitution of machines for labor, with output per miner tripling because of this in the two decades after 1950. The number of jobs open for coal miners fell drastically. Over 700,000 men were in the mines fifty years ago, compared to 135,000 today—a fall of over 80 percent.[7]

In recent years, many American unions have been considering important structural changes. Some want deeper involvement of unions in social problems, and more minority group membership. (The late Walter Reuther, former head of the C.I.O., took his United Auto Workers out of the A.F.L.-C.I.O. because of these and other issues in 1968.) Other unions have been pressing to organize professional workers, including teachers and other government employees. New forms of compensation have arisen, with fringe benefits (vacations, medical care, pension plans) rising in importance vis-à-vis the standard campaigns for higher wages and shorter hours.

Profit sharing plans (discussed in the final chapter) and cost-of-living adjustments to wage agreements, based on the consumer price index, have become more popular. So has industry-wide bargaining, where a few big firms or an employers' combine bargains with one or a few big unions in a

---

[7] In the first five years after the 1950 agreement, the number of jobs in coal mining fell by almost half.

"package deal."[8] Finally, the public and their representatives in Congress have become very concerned over the high costs of strikes. The direct cost of a walkout in a key industry—say, railroads—may be far outweighed by the huge social cost to businessmen and consumers not involved in the strike. Delivery schedules are disrupted, plants shut down, workers laid off all over the economy. The amount a railroad can save or workers can gain by winning a strike can be far less than the social costs felt by the economy at large.

With this in mind, proposals for compulsory arbitration of strikes of national importance have been frequently heard. Compulsory arbitration would require unions and management which cannot agree to submit their dispute to a neutral third party. The arbiter would then impose a solution. Opponents of arbitration argue that without the power of the strike no one, including the arbiter, can judge what bargain would be reached: a market solution is usurped by a fallible human. This argument is true, yet most strikes of national importance involve big unions against big management, so that a competitive market solution would not occur anyway. When this is considered along with the immense potential for social cost in work stoppages which affect the public, compulsory arbitration seems to make sense. Whatever the pros and cons, the idea has gained a great deal of support in recent years.

Questions

1. What have been the most important court decisions and legislation in the development of labor unions?
2. How do unions attempt to raise wages?
3. Should compulsory arbitration be adopted?

---

[8] Resembling the bilateral monopoly case discussed in chapter 12.

14.

TOPICS IN
INCOME DISTRIBUTION:
Rent, Interest, Profit

A general theory for determining factor incomes was developed in chapter 12. Although this theory applies to all the factors, there are some special points involving rent, interest, and profit which should be emphasized briefly.

RENT

The study of rent is one of the oldest in economics; ideas first published by David Ricardo in England between 1815 and 1821 still appear in modern texts. Thus far in this book we have spoken of rent as the return to the factor of production land. So it is, and so the term was always employed originally. But modern economists use a much broader definition which calls rent the return to *any* factor which cannot be reproduced.

This can best be explained by an example. Figure 14–1 shows supply and demand for a scarce and irreproducible factor. It might be a lot at the corner of Madison and State Streets in Chicago, music-making by the Beatles or Beethoven, the sports services of Bobby Orr, Johnnie Bench, or Brazil's Pele. All these examples earn "economic rent." The factor, whether Beethoven or Bench, will serve in its best alternative use (writing music, playing baseball) at any price above OP in Figure 14–1. Depending on the demand for the factor's services, the equilibrium price may be very high, or it may be near to OP. Any payment to the factor above OP will keep the factor employed full-time in its present use as shown by the vertical portion of the supply curve. The amount by which payment exceeds OP is called economic rent. Note on the diagram that a

FIGURE 14-1

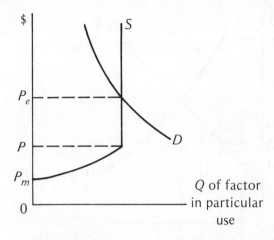

fall in price below OP will cause a factor to start transferring its services into another use. That transfer will be total if price drops to some minimum level OPm.

Almost always, there will be some economic rent being earned in any factor market. Figure 14-2 shows supply and demand for professors of economics. Equilibrium salary is OW. But note that at least one dedicated prof[1] would work for far less; a salary of OA would suffice to hire him. Professor number two could be hired for OB, number three for OC. But all get the market salary OW because competition bids their price up to that point. Hence professor number one gets economic rent equal to the red bar, number two's rent is shown by dotted bar, number three by a striped bar and number four by red stripes. Thus the total economic rent being earned is equivalent to the area above a factor's supply curve up to equilibrium price. Clearly, the flatter (more elastic) the supply curve, the less economic rent will accrue.

The theory of economic rent is the basis for the famous "single tax" proposal of Henry George, a 19th century American economist, whose book *Progress and Poverty* (1879) was wildly popular for many years. George proposed a simple plan. As factors earning economic rent will still work in the same occupation if they receive less, then tax away this surplus and

---

[1] *No doubt the very one of whom it is said "he never met a payroll," or "if you can't do, then teach."*

FIGURE 14–2

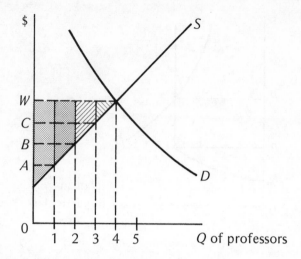

finance government spending with it.[2] As long as the tax does not exceed the rent component, no distortion of factor use will occur. George and his supporters were wrong in thinking a single tax on land above could replace all other taxes—it would not collect enough revenue—but many economists agree that increased taxation of economic rent in this country would indeed interfere less with factor use then would other forms of taxation.

INTEREST

In simple theory, our framework of supply and demand explains interest rates as well. There is a demand for loanable funds by businesses which want to invest, by households for consumer spending and mortgages, and by federal, state and local governments to finance spending. We expect that high interest rates will discourage borrowing, while lower interest rates stimulate it. The demand curve in Figure 14–3 is thus drawn with a downward slope.

There is also a supply of loanable funds emanating from banks, and from households and businesses willing to lend by

---

[2] *George supported a land tax, but a tax on any economic rent obeys the same logic.*

FIGURE 14–3

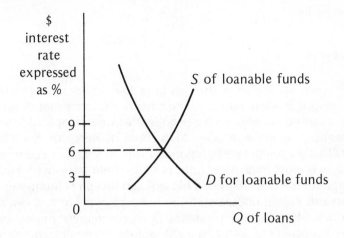

buying bonds. The supply curve in Figure 14–3 is upward sloping, signifying that greater quantities of loanable funds will be
available at higher interest rates. With supply and demand as
they are in the diagram, the market mechanism will cause an
equilibrium to occur at a 6 percent interest rate.

We all know that more than one interest rate exists in an
economy. There is a rate for long-term loans, and another for
short-term; one for government bonds and another for private; one for risky customers and another for the trustworthy;
one for borrowers from a bank and another for those who put
their funds into the bank to draw interest. Our diagram should
be interpreted as showing the situation for a safe, long-term
borrower. A premium will have to be added for risk, or for
short-term borrowers. On the other side of the coin, a bank
depositor will receive less than the indicated rate. A bank
makes its profit on the difference between the interest rate it
pays depositors and the higher rate it charges borrowers.

Interest rate theory is a complicated area of modern
economics, and more advanced books spend much time discussing Keynesian liquidity preference, discounted present
value, and so forth. Here it is sufficient to say that interest
rates, like other factor prices, can be looked at as a result of the
market forces of supply and demand. It must be remembered,
however, that governments interfere with the market for loanable funds on a continual basis. Monetary policy—the control

of inflation or depression by managing interest rates—involves exactly this.[3]

PROFIT

We have already seen that profit is the return to the entrepreneur that is left over after the costs of a firm are met. Among the many books which have been written on the topic of profit, attention should be directed to the body of literature which has justified the legitimate function of profit in a market economy. The two most important authors in the field have been Frank Knight of the University of Chicago, and Joseph Schumpeter of Harvard. Knight popularized the concept of profit as a reward for risk-taking by entrepreneurs. Every commercial project carries a prospect of gain and a risk of loss. Some entrepreneurs calculate markets, demand, costs, the odds, and government policy with acumen. Their reward is profit. Others are less shrewd and lose out. When losses are incurred, it is the entrepreneur who is responsible for making them good. As with Harry Truman, "the buck stops here." In short, profit is a form of income which in part is a reward for taking risks. Joseph Schumpeter added to our understanding of profit by calling attention to the entrepreneur's role as initiator and innovator. In any commercial project, someone must hatch new ideas and commence operations (initiation). More profit stands to be earned if new ways of doing things cut costs, lead to untapped markets, or alter the product in an appealing way (innovation).[4] Thus, said Schumpeter, profit can be seen as a return to the entrepreneur's initiating and innovating activities.

Taken together, the notions of Knight and Schumpeter lead us to the modern view of the entrepreneurial function: initiation, innovation, and risk-taking, with profit as the reward. The main lesson of this chapter has been the application of our general theory of how incomes are determined to rent, interest, and profit. Though there are many complications in each of these three areas, our supply and demand framework can still explain a great deal about these subjects.

---

[3] See chapters 8, 9, and 10 of the author's Managing the Modern Economy.

[4] Remember not to confuse innovation with invention. As we saw in chapter 2, invention is an act of fresh discovery. Innovation is the act of making inventions commercially useful. Many inventions never become business successes because innovation is not applied to them.

Questions

1. What is economic rent? How does it appear on a diagram?
2. How can supply and demand be used to explain interest rates?
3. What are the economic justifications for profit in a market system?

IV.

HOW TO ACHIEVE ECONOMIC GROWTH IN A MARKET ECONOMY

15.

THE EXPERIENCE OF THE US AND THE LESSONS OF OTHER COUNTRIES

This chapter will examine the last of the four critical questions that an economic system must answer: How are the decisions made which relate to economic growth?

A simple definition of economic growth is a rise in *real gross national product* over time. Real gross national product is defined as the money value of a year's output of goods and services, corrected for inflation. For a full explanation including the dangers of equating GNP with welfare, and the difficulties of measurement, see chapters 2 and 3 of *Managing the Modern Economy*. Leaving these questions aside, what promotes growth in real GNP? Economists view growth as the outcome of changes in the "production function" relating growth to its determinants. There is wide agreement that improvement in the following categories promotes growth:

1. Amount and quality of labor, including skills, health, and length of work week.

2. Amount and quality of land, including natural resources.

3. Amount and quality of capital, including technical change, transportation, and marketing facilities.

4. Amount and quality of entrepreneurial input.

5. Economies of scale as limited by the size of the market.

6. Psychological, cultural, and social change.

Note that many of the items listed are subject to market influences. That is, if a working man sees that he can better his income by more education, then there is an economic incentive in the market system for him to return to school. The lure of profit helps in developing new supplies of natural resources. The potential for profit also motivates businessmen to invest in new capital (plant and equipment), and to search for technical improvements. Profit leads the budding entrepreneur to the Harvard Business School. And it also is the incentive for exploiting economies of scale. The market system thus has a built-in motivation for private reward.

The six elements in the growth process just mentioned are very broad. Easy formulas predicting growth on the basis of change in one or more key areas are not to be expected. At one time, there was overwhelming concentration on capital formation as the critical factor in the developmental process. Early attempts to derive simple growth equations led to great popularity for one such theory, the Harrod-Domar capital-output ratio.[1] But these conceptions were not particularly helpful because recent studies have tended to show that exclusive concern with the quantity of capital conceals more about growth than it reveals. Pioneering efforts by economist Edward Denison to quantify the contribution of all elements in US growth during the period 1909–1957 show that education is as important as capital formation. Three other elements—economies of scale, improvement in technology, and the beneficial effect of shorter hours on labor productivity—when taken together are estimated to be more than twice as important as capital in explaining growth.[2] Research of this type is beset with pitfalls and this data should be taken with a grain of salt. But enough is now known to assure us that growth is no simple, easily explained process with the sheer quantity of capital as the paramount factor.

The long-term record of US economic growth has been quite good since the Civil War. In the century after that conflict, real GNP grew annually at 3.6 percent, second only to Japan (3.8

---

[1] Sir Roy Harrod of Oxford and Evsey Domar of Harvard developed the theory that changes in GNP have a direct mathematical relation to capital formulation. These two excellent economists are not responsible for the unproductive uses of their equations in the past two decades.

[2] Denison's research was divided into the periods 1909–1929, and 1929–1957. Capital accumulation per se was more important in the earlier period than in the later period.

percent) and far ahead of Germany's 2.8 percent, Britain's 1.9 percent, and France's 1.7 percent among major market economies. The lead is not so great when corrected for population growth (per capita income) but the record is still outstanding. However, US growth performance over the last ten years has been much poorer, averaging only 2.7 percent in real terms and ranking ahead of only Britain among the nations just mentioned.

WHAT CAN WE LEARN FROM THE EXPERIENCE OF OTHER COUNTRIES?

The Scottish poet Robert Burns once wrote three lines worth a whole philosophy course: "O wad some Power the giftie gie us to see oursels as ithers see us! It wad frae monie a blunder free us, an foolish notion." In this spirit, we can ask what other market economies have to teach us concerning economic growth. The pattern followed will be to go down our list of factors promoting growth (on page 180), calling attention to countries where things are done differently and where we might have something to learn.

Programs Affecting Labor

In some countries, government policy has been geared to the encouragement of labor mobility. Labor can easily find itself locked into declining industries or areas due to lack of the right skills, lack of knowledge about job openings elsewhere, and insufficient personal funds to support a search for new housing in another community which all contribute to low mobility.

Sweden has tackled these problems more seriously than has any other western nation. A joint government-labor-management agency called the National Labor Market Board supervises comprehensive policies which encourage workers to transfer from low to high productivity employment. At the heart of the program is the N.L.M.B. information/education system. Through 24 regional and over 600 local employment offices, knowledge of job openings is disseminated widely, aided by a 60-page weekly gazette with national coverage. Expenses are paid in a variety of retraining courses which often allow the student to continue working at his old job while studying for a new one. There are generous relocation and travel allowances for workers making a move. Travel and living expenses involved in job hunting are subsidized, stipends are provided for settlement costs, and the N.L.M.B. will even buy a worker's old house if he cannot find a buyer for it in a declining area.

In other countries, union structure has undergone changes in recent years which apparently promote growth. The German case deserves most attention. Built from scratch after Germany's collapse in World War II, German unions are much better suited to modern industrial conditions than are Great Britain's, for example. A high degree of mutual understanding with management exists on the question of introducing labor-saving machinery and reallocating labor to more productive roles. There are only a few large unions, no jurisdictional disputes, and a proclivity to avoid strikes as socially harmful except as a rare last resort. German unions also support, with business and management, a large-scale national apprenticeship program and system of trade schools. After eight or nine grades of elementary school, many young people enter privately-run government-subsidized technical training institutions. Large firms administer their own apprenticeship programs, while small ones contribute to special programs run by chambers of commerce. Apprentices must attend weekly classes until age 18. German unions thus receive an inflow of trained personnel who are very useful in promoting growth.[3]

In Sweden, trade unions push up wages enthusiastically, and leave management free to lay off labor if this means greater efficiency. Recently the union concerned with the Swedish shoe industry made the announcement, startling to an American, that if the industry could not compete against imports, it should be shut down and its labor and other resources transferred to more productive uses. Union economists possess a refreshing tendency to view job security not as lifetime tenure in the same slot, but instead as a guarantee of employment though not necessarily in the same industry.

Another interesting effort to improve the productivity of labor has been worker participation in management and profit sharing. The idea of systematically appointing workers as

---

[3] *The study of foreign languages is emphasized in these programs. The excellent English of many young workers, and almost universally in the telephone and telegraph services, is no coincidence.*

members of boards of directors first arose in Germany and Yugoslavia.[4] In Germany, such labor representatives have served on management boards in the coal and steel industries since 1951. The system has since been expanded so that all corporations with over 500 employees must by law give a third of their board seats to worker representatives (in coal and steel the proportion is 50–50), and the majority rules in making decisions. Called *mitbestimmung* (voting together), the system is believed to have improved industrial relations by giving workers real responsibility in company direction, and by keeping labor and management in constant contact with each other's thinking.[5]

1973 was a big year for the concept of worker-directors. Norway introduced them by law in January, 1973, Sweden in February, Denmark decided to adopt the practice in 1975, and Britain is considering the idea. The Netherlands has a different type of plan: although there are no labor members on boards, under a new law of July, 1973, workers have veto power over any board appointment. Even the commissioners of the European Common Market have bought the idea. In 1972 they called for member nations still without worker participation to adopt a plan based on either the Dutch or the German model.

In France, profit sharing has received more attention than worker-management. The late Charles de Gaulle had pushed since 1958 for worker partnership in profits. Under a law of 1967, applying to firms with over 100 employees, a portion of profits determined by a complicated formula is paid to workers, usually in the form of stock. The stock cannot be sold for five years, so that the funds represented have to remain invested in the company for that period.

Programs Affecting Capital Investment

One common criticism of the untrammeled market system is that growth may be too fast or too slow. Entrepreneurs make

---

[4] Yugoslavia's "worker-management" will be considered in a subsequent volume.

[5] There are some who believe that worker representation would make it impossible to lay off employees when an industry is in decline. Germany's coal and steel industries are evidence to the contrary. With labor in half the board seats, 400,000 jobs have nevertheless been eliminated over the past 20 years with no difficulty. Worker-directors have supported liberal severance pay and an organized search for new jobs, rather than stone-walling against layoffs.

their investment decisions solely on the basis of expected private profit, whereas externalities may be present which suggest faster growth to improve living standards, or slower growth to avoid environmental problems. Indeed, any time social costs and benefits differ from private costs and benefits, then we may expect the amount of capital investment to be "wrong" from a social point of view.

This is the background to the various types of investment planning found today.[6] "Comprehensive" or "heavy" plans with aggregate mathematical models and strict overall government control on private investment are entirely confined to countries of the underdeveloped world. An analysis of comprehensive planning will thus be postponed to a forthcoming volume on international trade and economic development.

However, several market economies have opted for another type of planning which deserves investigation. This is the concept of "indicative planning" used by France since shortly after World War II, and now found in several countries with French ties, in Spain, and to some extent in Japan. Indicative planning is deceptively simple; its basis is a giant market research mechanism organized by government and freely available to the public. The idea is to influence the decisions of companies by ensuring that all are aware of the same very detailed economic predictions for all sectors of the economy. Familiarity with indicative planning can be gained by looking at the steps in the French mechanism:

1. Long before the start of the planning year, French political authorities decide on general aims to be pursued: modernization of the economy, full employment, an attack on social costs, promotion of social benefits, and so on. Given these political decisions, a projected rate of growth in GNP is announced. The rate chosen takes into account the avoidance of both inflation and unemployment; 5.9 percent is the figure for the planning period 1971–75.

2. After the overall projection is made, the planning agency (named the *Commission du Plan*) then takes over, drawing up sectoral growth targets for each of 28 sectors of the economy. Government spending is already projected (see step #1

---

[6] *In less developed countries, other common justifications for planning are ignorance and lack of information among private investors, the presence of monopoly elements, a socially undesirable maldistribution of income, and a private unwillingness to invest large sums because of a great preference for present consumption. None of these arguments is used very often to advocate planning for developed market economies, however.*

above). Given this, estimates are then made of maximum feasible private consumption which can be sustained in each sector at the growth rate selected. The planners then project the levels of investment, raw materials, and other inputs needed to hit the growth targets. Taking all these together, a forecast can now be made for all sectors of production.

3. At this point, sectoral committees (*Commissions de Modernisation*) take over. Composed of 30 to 50 members representing government and business, these committees make detailed product analyses predicting demand, output, and input requirements within their sector.[7] Inter-sector coordinating committees help to obtain consistency in the sectoral predictions, avoiding embarrassments such as the iron and steel sector planning a 3 percent growth in steel output while other sectors plan for 5 percent greater steel input. After consistency is obtained, the *Commission du Plan* compiles all the targets in total and by sector, and publishes them as the Plan. Then the whole package goes for approval to the French National Assembly.

The expectation is that private firms will base their investment and output decisions on the information embodied in the plan. Obviously, if firms believe that the Plan's predictions are accurate and act accordingly, then the predictions will turn out to be correct! Indicative planning thus relies heavily on the doctrine of "self-fulfilling prophecy" to achieve its aims.

The Plan in principle involves neither the obligation to follow it nor sanctions against businessmen who ignore it (which is why it is called indicative). The whole structure could thus be a house of cards, liable to tumble down if people lose confidence in its predictions. However, behind the scenes the French government can bring very strong influence to bear on the business community. There are two reasons why we may expect reasonable accuracy in the Plan's projections:

1. The French government is both a big employer (over 25 percent of the non-farm labor force) and a big investor (over one third of all gross investment). The largest single sector of the economy can therefore be depended on not to ignore its targets.

2. For the private sector, a mix of government policies may be used to influence and persuade recalcitrant entrepreneurs.

---

[7] *Except for large nationalized enterprises, projections are not on a firm-by-firm basis.*

Eight major types of tax relief are available for this purpose, the most important of which is the power to suspend taxes on dividends for seven years when new investment approved by the planning authorities is undertaken. In a country where taxation of corporate profits is relatively high, this becomes a lure which few firms can afford to overlook. In the area of private credit, entrepreneurs have to get government permission for new bond issues. A wide range of subsidies may be paid to firms willing to increase exports, or planning to retool with modern equipment. Controls over the location of new industry attempt to shift the economic base away from booming regions such as the Paris region and the south coast, toward more backward areas (Brittany, the Pas de Calais, etc.). On occasion, discriminatory use of price controls and advertising on government TV have been used to protect the Plan. Finally, there is always the possibility that official contracts may be withheld from selected firms which refuse to abide by planning goals. Although not used to the extent they might be, the mere existence of these weapons must be taken into account by any French businessman. Incidentally, Charles de Gaulle was not a great supporter of indicative planning, although the mechanism seems to have recovered its standing since his death.

It is difficult to assess the results of French indicative planning. Sometimes plan predictions have been borne out in real growth, sometimes the targets have been missed. The greatest accuracy was achieved in the fourth planning period, 1962–65, when the projected GNP growth of 5.5 percent was attained exactly. The present sixth plan is also doing very well, with actual growth over the last three years (5.8 percent) only .1 percent off the predicted 5.9 percent.[8]

Evidence also suggests that French growth has shown more stability over time than has been true in the US, and that efficiency has been promoted by holding down the level of unutilized industrial capacity. Some hostile observers believe that French-style planning has an inherent tendency to lead to market-sharing between established firms. When new firms and new innovations come along, these must be repressed or planning inaccuracies will result. Still, the Plan does give im-

---

[8] *The fifth plan, by contrast, was a flop. It was wrecked by the political turmoil of May, 1968, and the currency crisis which hit the franc in 1969; the plan missed its targets by wide margins.*

mense publicity to economic forecasts, leading to more knowledgeable and more serious public debate than in many other countries. Finally, there seems to be more business, labor, and voter acceptance of unpalatable measures when they are tied concretely to the Plan. Thus the government finds it useful to clothe its fiscal and monetary assaults against inflation as planning defenses.

Japan uses a modified sort of indicative planning. The most striking element in the Japanese use of the idea is the very close liaison between its first-rate government bureaucracy and business management. In fact, the same people often serve in both capacities at different times in their lives due to the peculiar Japanese civil service system which attracts the best talents Japan has to offer. University graduates in the civil service all move step-by-step to higher positions as their seniority grows. By long established custom, when all are in their late 40s, one talented member of that age group is promoted to vice-minister of a particular department (the minister is a political appointee). Again by tradition, most of his contemporaries in the department will resign, but their careers are far from blighted. Almost immediately they move into responsible positions on the boards of directors of banks, industrial corporations, trading firms, and the like. Especially desirable are "graduates" of the Ministry of Trade and Industry (M.I.T.I.), who provide firms with very high quality talent and who themselves maintain close contacts with the planning authorities. Meanwhile, the planners now have many old colleagues in the world of business, with whom they have considerable rapport, not least because these businessmen understand the problems of economic management. These close connections are one element in the remarkable success story of Japanese growth.

Japan's indicative plan, like France's, emphasizes data collection and great publicity for official predictions, with taxes and subsidies available for influence if targets are being missed. It appears that greater efforts are made than in France to keep information current, with updated plan estimates for the next year forthcoming frequently. There is a census of manufacturing every year, and of commerce every two years (more often than in the US,) while M.I.T.I. stands ready to undertake sample surveys of markets whenever there is a demand for its services. The government watches productivity figures closely, and it is M.I.T.I. policy to identify declining industries, and to help push the factors employed there into more profitable enterprises. All this is not confined to domestic markets, either. Government studies of foreign demand and foreign output patterns are also made, and the information gleaned from this research can be of great help to potential exporters.[9] Sweden does not have an annual development plan. However, it does make use of some interesting government controls over growth. No new firm can build and no existing firm can expand its facilities without applying for a construction license issued by the Swedish government.[10] These licenses can be used when needed to alter the direction of growth. For example, a license may be granted rapidly for construction in backward northern areas, while delayed or denied for southern areas with pollution problems.

As distinct from planning and controls, some countries have adopted innovations increasing the amount of private saving, which can then be used to fund capital investment by businesses. Germany has a government scheme to encourage saving by depositing in a saver's bank account a "matching grant"—usually 20 percent, but as high as 35 percent for building and loan societies. To qualify, savings must be left on deposit for from five to six years. These long-term accounts also draw regular interest from the banks.

Sweden uses a similar tool, but applies it to businesses only. Firms are encouraged by tax incentives to set aside up to 40 percent of their before tax earnings as an investment reserve. This reserve, kept on deposit in the banking system, is free of all tax. After five years, 30 percent of it may be used without strings. The rest of the reserve is released for use periodically when Swedish authorities move to combat an economic downturn. If the reserve is spent without permission, the maverick firm is subject to the tax originally avoided, plus a 10 percent penalty.

Japan encourages private saving by a very unusual method —the semi-annual bonus. Every six months or so, almost half the wages of a Japanese employee are paid over as a lump sum. Similarly, pensions are commonly settled in one big payment. Note the interesting result: liquid funds accumulate in the

---

[9] At present, the US government does very little along these lines.

[10] For years, permits were needed for machinery as well as buildings, but this is no longer true.

banking system as firms save to make the payments, while after they are made workers have swollen bank accounts for some time as they slowly spend their bonus. The net result is a boost to net savings deposits in banks, compared to countries which pay wages and salaries on a weekly or monthly basis. In turn, investment is promoted.

Programs Affecting Entrepreneurial Quality

Germany, as befits its new reputation as an economic titan, has a noteworthy policy which appears to improve entrepreneurship at the level of the firm. This is the *aufsichtsrat* or supervisory board, an old corporate institution which became more important after World War II. Historically, the *aufsichtsrat* came into being to give more power to shareholders of a firm. It is a standing committee which supervises corporate managers much more closely than can the annual meeting of stockholders. Large stockholders, particularly the big German banking houses such as Deutsche Bank, Dresdner Bank, and Commerzbank are influential on these boards.[11] Their representatives have a unique opportunity to compare efficiency and entrepreneurship between industries, and among firms within an industry. They also have a motive to do so, for better management will mean more dividends for stockholders. It is thus common to find representatives of the same bank on the supervisory board of a firm which is the most poorly run in its industry, and on another firm which is the most efficient. The interchange of information does appear to be significant in improving the general level of entrepreneurship.[12]

The author does not necessarily advocate the immediate or outright adoption of any of these policies for stimulating and controlling growth. However, he does feel that there is a great deal to be learned from the experience of other countries. Not nearly enough study has been done in the US by government, by business, or by academic economists, to sift these ideas. Some of them might wither in the American economic climate. But some might thrive.

---

[11] *Particularly so because of the German custom whereby small shareholders usually deposit their stock with their bank, giving the bank a proxy to vote these shares at stockholders meetings.*

[12] *Japan has a somewhat similar system.*

Questions

1. Discuss the policies and programs encountered abroad which affect the labor force.
2. What is indicative planning? How does it work in France? In Japan?
3. How does Germany affect entrepreneurial policy?
4. Do you think any of the ideas discussed in this chapter would be beneficial for the United States? Why or why not?

16.

RESUME

From the earliest times, man has lived under an economic system which answers the four basic economic questions: what to produce, by what methods to produce it, how to allocate the goods produced among the members of society, and how to achieve economic growth. The major ways these questions have been approached are through the traditional economy, the command economy such as now used by most Marxist countries, and the market system.

The market system, a term more accurate than its alternatives "capitalism" and "free enterprise," uses prices and profits to answer the basic questions. What is produced depends on interaction between buyers who establish a demand for goods, and sellers who want to maximize profits. A seller will need to know the revenue he can earn from sales, and his costs of production, in order to calculate his maximum profit level of output. The techniques of production will also be determined by the search for profit, because if costs are allowed to rise over their minimum level, then profits will be reduced. Who gets the goods in greatest quantity? Those who have earned the most income by selling factors of production (land, labor, capital, and entrepreneurial ability) to producers at the highest prices.

Under perfect competition, the market system possesses striking advantages of efficiency. The conjunction of market demand and supply determine an equilibrium price, which is the measure of scarcity or abundance of a commodity. Government interference with equilibrium, as in price controls, maximum rent and interest laws, agricultural price supports, and minimum wages, although perhaps useful otherwise causes predictable shortages or surpluses to develop.

Perfect competition also tends to eliminate any abnormal profits, as firms enter an industry to share in the high returns. Competition thus enforces production at minimum cost per unit of output. Taken together, these two attributes mean that the consumer is charged the lowest price for the product consistent with a firm's survival. This pleasant outlook has to be altered, however, when firms have the power to control their price. "Imperfections" in the market may be caused by economies of scale too large to permit more than one or a few firms to exist in a market, by public utility regulation and patents, by superior entrepreneurship, by control of essential resources, or by high cost barriers, particularly advertising, which make entry into an industry difficult. The case of only one firm in an industry—monopoly—is simple to analyze. To maximize profits it will select a higher price and a lower quantity of output than would be true under competition. More commonly, market power is found in two other forms: monopolistic competition and oligopoly. Under monopolistic competition, entry into an industry is free enough so that abnormal profits are eventually competed away. However, firms can seize short-run profit by differentiating their product through advertising or quality change. Although competitors will respond with their own ads and quality change, a temporary advantage will accrue to the first firm. Thus product differentiation is rational from the businessman's point of view. Oligopoly—a small number of firms in an industry—is less predictable because the actions of any one firm must be taken into account by the others. Such "mutual dependence" often leads to collusion, price leadership, and a basic unwillingness to compete in terms of price. On the other hand, oligopolies are able to generate economies of scale. They also have the profits to finance extensive research, although evidence shows that small firms and independent inventors do very well by comparison.

The US government has traditionally tried to control market power by use of antitrust regulations. The Sherman Act of 1890 and the Clayton Act of 1914 are the bases for attacking monopoly. However, in spite of the precedent of a few court decisions, many forms of oligopolistic behavior are not now prosecuted by the Justice Department, and antitrust law is not the factor it might be in American economic life.

In one other area, the optimistic predictions of perfect competition may not be borne out. When social costs and benefits diverge from private costs and benefits, then decisions in the market place will be less advantageous to society. Several methods are available for closing this divergence; for example, direct controls, taxes, and subsidies. Serious difficulties in estimating the dollar value of social costs and benefits, however, have not yet been overcome.

The setting of prices and the presence or absence of competition is paralleled in the area of income distribution among the factors of production. The supply of a factor and its demand determine its equilibrium price. The demand for a factor is a bit complex, however, as it is derived from the desire to produce output. Thus a businessman must consider the physical product of a factor, and the price at which the output produced by that factor can be sold, which together allow him to determine how much revenue will be earned from their use. Knowing factor cost, he can now hire the quantity of factors which will maximize profit.

Imperfections are possible in markets for factors as well as in product markets. Labor unions (factor monopolies) may engineer wages higher than equilibrium, while big employers with control over labor markets (factor monopsonies) may force lower wages on workers. When a factor monopoly faces a factor monopsony, the situation is called bilateral monopoly and the outcome is indeterminate, being based wholly on the bargaining strength and tactics of the parties involved.

The resume thus far has considered the market system's response to the questions what to produce, by what manner to produce them, and how to distribute the output once it is produced. The last great question facing the economy is how to achieve growth. In an unconstrained market system, growth is a by-product of the search for profits. Because US growth rates in recent years have been behind many other market economies, attention has naturally focused on the growth experience of these countries. Many novel programs affecting labor mobility, union activity, worker participation in management, saving and investment, and entrepreneurship are in successful operation elsewhere. Some of them might prove useful for this country, and it would be short-sighted to overlook or to ignore these experiences.